WAIT DON'T SIGN THAT NIL CONTRACT

WAIT DON'T SIGN THAT NIL CONTRACT

GO-TO GUIDE FOR THE COLLEGIATE ATHLETE AND THEIR FAMILIES FOR NIL MONEY

Jonathan Miller, CPA
with Taylor Madwin

JONES MEDIA
PUBLISHING

Wait Don't Sign That NIL Contract: The Go-To Guide for the Collegiate Athlete and their families for NIL Money
Copyright © 2024 by Jonathan Miller

Jones Media Publishing
10645 N. Tatum Blvd. Ste. 200-166
Phoenix, AZ 85028
www.JonesMediaPublishing.com

Disclaimer:

The author strives to be as accurate and complete as possible in the creation of this book, notwithstanding the fact that the author does not warrant or represent at any time that the contents within are accurate due to the rapidly changing nature of the Internet.

While all attempts have been made to verify information provided in this publication, the Author and the Publisher assume no responsibility and are not liable for errors, omissions, or contrary interpretation of the subject matter herein. The Author and Publisher hereby disclaim any liability, loss or damage incurred as a result of the application and utilization, whether directly or indirectly, of any information, suggestion, advice, or procedure in this book. Any perceived slights of specific persons, peoples, or organizations are unintentional.

In practical advice books, like anything else in life, there are no guarantees of income made. Readers are cautioned to rely on their own judgment about their individual circumstances to act accordingly. Readers are responsible for their own actions, choices, and results. This book is not intended for use as a source of legal, business, accounting or financial advice. All readers are advised to seek the services of competent professionals in legal, business, accounting, and finance field.

Printed in the United States of America

ISBN: 978-1-948382-69-4 paperback

Contents

Introduction

Congratulations! You have just been given the opportunity and freedom to use and manage your own name, image, and likeness, or "NIL."

The National Collegiate Athletic Association (NCAA) is currently in the midst of a major shift in its policy regarding the rights of student athletes to receive payment for the use of their name, image, and likeness (NIL). For years, the NCAA has prohibited athletes from earning money, but that is now changing. As a student-athlete, you are now able to create and manage your own brand, establish partnerships, sponsorship deals, sign with a sports agent and profit off of your NIL.

In June of 2021, the NCAA Board of Governors voted unanimously to begin the process of allowing student athletes to benefit from the use of their name, image, and likeness. This decision came as a result of the landmark Supreme Court case, NCAA v Alston, which ruled in favor of the student athlete for the first time in the history of collegiate athletics with regard to NIL.

This new landscape of college athletics has been difficult to navigate as it is unprecedented and unclear. Boundaries and parameters for NIL have not been specified by the NCAA explicitly, so, in this book, we will help you to understand the intricacies of NIL and its great effect on amateur athletics.

The NCAA's new stance on NIL is a major step forward for student athletes, who have long been denied the opportunity to benefit from their own name, image, and likeness. While the NCAA has yet to set any specific rules or regulations regarding NIL, it is clear that the organization is committed to creating a fair system. The member organization has stated that it will consult with its member schools, the student-athletes, and other stakeholders to ensure that any changes to the policy are fair and equitable. NIL is going to be a major game-changer for collegiate athletics and will ultimately revolutionize the entire sports landscape.

The NIL environment is constantly changing and adapting and it will likely change again by the time you finish this book. However, regardless of those specific rules and regulations, the purpose of this book is to help you figure out what to do with the money that you may be earning today. Balancing school and athletics are already a full-time job. Educating yourself on NIL, finances and life after college can sound daunting and unnecessary at this stage in your life. Through this book we hope to illustrate how best to manage this newfound opportunity most notably the potential to earn money. We hope to answer questions that may come with your NIL opportunities such as...

- What are the intricacies of the new NIL landscape, how is it being implemented, and how has the landscape changed since the early 2000's?
- Where does the money come from?
- What are the threats to NIL and college sports?
- What questions should you ask when signing a deal?
- What does it mean to have ownership and control of your name, image and likeness?
- What are your rights and how do you protect them?
- What are your tax obligations on theincome you receive?

The answers to these questions are not necessarily clear. Additionally, the NCAA has not done their due diligence in educating student-athletes on the NIL landscape. While some schools are offering educational seminars for their student-athletes on NIL, these decisions can and will affect your future careers and lives. It is imperative that you know how to navigate NIL before jumping in head-first.

Once again, congratulations on your successes and we hope this book can help ease the transition into this new NIL-led collegiate athletics world.

Chapter 1

NIL

Hey there! If you are reading this, you are probably between the ages of 16 and 22 years old and asking, "Why do I need to know this?" Perhaps you are a parent, family member, mentor, or advisor of the a 16 to 22-year-old student athlete trying to understand how to navigate NIL as well. Maybe you are a former student athlete trying to understand how these changes are being enforced or looking to learn how to manage life after your career. This book is for all of you! It is important to educate yourselves on the changing landscape of collegiate athletics and we are here to help you do exactly that.

The following are in depth answers to the most commonly asked questions with regard to NIL.

What are the intricacies of the new NIL landscape and how has the landscape changed since the early 2000's?

With the aforementioned drastic changes to the landscape of college football, student athletes are now able to profit off of their name image and likeness. This means student athletes can sign endorsement and marketing deals and profit off of their name and likeness if they desire. Players have never had this opportunity before. In fact, student athletes and Universities, most notably Reggie Bush and the University of Southern California in 2009, have been severely punished for disregarding NCAA rules regarding paying players. This is no longer the case. It is the duty of each university to regulate NIL however most are looking at NIL changes as an asset to provide student athletes with financial opportunities. Yet they still have the responsibility to provide information to students that is critical to navigating this new opportunity.

There are many opportunities for student athletes because of these NIL changes. Student athletes, especially those performing at a very high level in the most popular sports at the most well-known schools, are able to profit off of their personal brand. They can do this by signing partnership deals, selling apparel, coaching sports camps, entrepreneurship, appearances and autographs sessions. Some players have signed deals with local businesses for social media marketing. Stetson Bennett, Quarterback for the University of Georgia, worked the drive-through line at Raising Canes following the Bulldogs 65-7 National Championship win. LSU gymnast, Olivia Dunne, has gained a following on TikTok with 7.2 million followers and has earned over a million dollars in revenue from her social media presence. Caleb Williams, 2022 Heisman Trophy Winner and USC Quarterback, has three massive NIL deals including one with Fanatics where he profits off selling officially licensed CW memorabilia. These are just a few examples of how student-athletes are now able to use their name, image, and likeness to their advantage. It is important to note that student-athletes are still not allowed to receive financial assistance from any university or college or anyone related to the schools. Simply put, NIL cannot be used for recruitment advantages, although it is apparent most universities are doing so. There are dangers that come with NIL and the lack of constraints the NCAA and the government have put on it, recruiting violations being one of those larger concerns.

There are five ways that universities are implementing NIL initiatives and offering these services to their student-athletes.

1. Collectives

   Collectives, as briefly mentioned earlier on in this chapter, are non-university sanctioned member groups who provide money to athletes through partnerships and brand deals. The only explicit rule regarding collectives is that boosters cannot directly pay these players to attend a certain school. This has become a point of contention with regard to college recruiting, especially in football and basketball, While NIL money may not necessarily be directly involved in recruiting athletes, schools that have the ability to offer players more money may have a better chance of successfully recruiting.

2. Local Marketing

   Local businesses have capitalized on using local players as a internet influencers for various brands of athletic drinks, sports equipment, clothes and other products this offers student-athletes to earn money from the comfort of their dorm room. The work is often in the form of appearances, videos, and social media posts, which they are able to do in their short amounts of free time.

3. Player-led marketplace

    Players are also now allowed to pursue entrepreneurship whether that be creating their own merchandise, starting their own businesses, or capitalizing on their social media presence in becoming an influencer.

4. Student-athlete empowerment

    Student athletes have banded together to fight for their right to profit off their name, image, and likeness.

5. The Metaverse

    The Metaverse, including NFT's and other crypto based products are yet untapped and unknown at this point. But may become a larger part of the NIL universe. Twitch and other platforms also allow players to be paid to "play" video games with fans, expanding fan engagement.

While these are all functional and pro-competitive ways for athletes to make money and build their brand, the NCAA is under enormous pressure to create and enforce real bylaws that these student-athletes can follow with regard to monetizing their NIL. Prior to the United States Supreme Court ruling in favor of student-athletes in NCAA v Alston, and states like California, Texas, and Florida subsequently created laws in favor of NIL monetization The NCAA faced a number of lawsuits which came from college student-athletes claiming antitrust violations by their respective schools, but no real change occurred until now. The fact that pendulum has swung so far the other way, allowing players to profit through university collectives, local business partnerships, entrepreneurial opportunities with no real parameters, is arguably more dangerous than anticipated. With even more questions than answers regarding NIL, it would be expected that the NCAA would create rules to ensure their student-athletes were protected and further lawsuits would not be necessary. Regardless, to ensure athletes are protected through this process of understanding the 'wild, wild, west' (unprecedented NIL world), education is critical.

What are the threats to the 'Wild, Wild, West'?

NIL is an entirely new landscape that gets discovered more and more each day. Most universities have dedicated time and resources to make NIL opportunities possible for its athletes. However, with power comes responsibility, making it imperative to analyze possible threats.

To begin, many people have questions about the longevity of NIL and its implications regarding an athletes' amateur status. In this emerging space, there are no consistent rules as each state has its own regulations and its own laws. TThis is creating current issues with recruiting even as the NCAA has conducted investigations in the past with illegal recruiting violations. While booster initiatives may be legal in some states, there are a myriad of states that constitute this behavior as illegal. This could create issues between the states and the NCAA as a whole, making the playing field significantly more uneven. For example, in Delaware, the Secretary of State has an approval process for those who are looking to be an "agent of student-athletes". This ensures that their money, time, and actions are best being used to support the athlete in a way that agrees with the NCAA and the state. On the other hand, states like Colorado are looking to follow the

NCAA and its defined rules (Dorner, 2023). Each University's compliance department is dealing with situations where every state has different laws, making collegiate athletics less uniform and more chaotic. In fact, these differing state laws leads to questions the impact NIL is already having on the recruiting landscape.

With the varying state laws, NIL is creating a stronger disparity in recruiting. Since NIL rules were enacted we have seen many top athletes entering the transfer portal to find the best financial opportunity for themselves. This unintended consequence has already created a division between the large D1 institutions and their donors versus smaller D1 institutions. Athletes are transferring schools more frequently because they are being offered more money and endorsements at other universities. Therefore, it is extremely important that the compliance department of each school is able to evaluate how to use NIL opportunities to market their school to recruits. This is something that is creating even more uncertainty as evidenced the ending of the PAC-12. By conducting research, working with coaches, advisors and the university collective, schools can find the best way to market the whole student-athlete experience. While the future may be unknown, many school's compliance departments are having to find ways to prepare for the continuing opportunities of NIL–despite its possible threats.

NIL has become a major concern for universities creating both the positive and negative financial implications. Most university athletic departments rely on donors and other fundraising to provide funding for their athletes. Unlike professional sports, college athletic departments want to spend as much money to improve the experience for their athletes. On average at a major university will spend $150,000 per student. This figure does not include other money which allows the university to pay student athletes for academic success which can add an average of $2 million per year per university. Legalizing NIL is great for the student athlete, however it has caused headaches for the athletic department's finances. It has increased their operating budgets and has created a competition for money from their donor base through collectives. There is now causing universities to look at "replacement dollars" which occurs when these donors shift their donations away from the athletic department to provide money for deals with student athletes via the collective. Naturally if this was allowed to occur it would present multiple issues for the financing of the athletic department. It is fortunate that the NCAA has stated that it is legal for Universities to have some oversight of the collectives and the source of the money paid to the athlete.

Where is the money coming from?

- You may be able to build your own NIL value through social media. Some athletes have a social media following and have used that to generate income. For example, Haley and Hanna Cavinder used their social media presence to gain a following and are now signing partnership deals left and right.

- Other athletes are capitalizing on their athletic prowess getting paid through advertising, appearances or sponsorship deals. Although it is technically not allowed for student-athletes to profit solely based on their on-field/court performance, typically the better you are at your sport, the more publicity you are able to generate. This is understandably appealing to anyone trying to sign a deal with you.

- Most often though, colleges and universities use NIL Collectives to turn a profit for their student-athletes. These collectives will gather money from boosters and businesses to essentially pay their student-athletes. The collectives must be completely independent of the university, however, in reality most of them are not. Because of the lack of parameters surrounding NIL for student-athletes, it has not been an issue for current athletes as of yet.

- However, collectives are starting to become infamous with regard to NIL and recruiting. People are speculating that boosters are pooling money and using it to recruit high school players under the guise of an "NIL deal" upon arrival on campus.

Potential ways to make money that are more niche:

1. Sign endorsement deals: College athletes can legally sign endorsement deals with companies or brands to promote their products and services.

2. Offer private lessons: College athletes can offer private lessons in their sport to younger athletes looking to improve their skills.

3. Sell merchandise: College athletes can create and sell their own merchandise such as t-shirts, hats, and other apparel.

4. Become a coach: College athletes can become a coach or instructor in their sport and teach younger athletes.

5. Offer tutoring services: College athletes can offer tutoring services in their area of expertise.

6. Become a speaker: College athletes can become a speaker and give motivational talks or lectures.

7. Become an influencer: College athletes can become influencers and promote products and services on social media.

8. Freelance: College athletes can freelance and offer services such as writing, web design, graphic design, etc.

9. Become a consultant: College athletes can become a consultant and offer advice to other athletes or teams.

10. Sell photos: College athletes can appear for autographs or sell autographed photos or sports cards.

Now, over a year since these changes, we are presented with a new, uncharted playing field. Due to the absence of nationally standardized rules and regulations regarding NIL policies around the country, this new playing field is a bit like the wild, wild west. Although the NIL landscape has no standardization at the moment, we get the extremely valuable and unparalleled opportunity to observe how many different organizational, institutional, and agency NIL models, provide different avenues which can be utilized to maximize player monetization while still generating revenue for the school. By looking at the widely varied models implemented across states, schools and conferences schools are able to create a personalized NIL model that is optimized to each university's unique market, network, strengths, and weaknesses.

Besides the differences in monetization opportunities based on school, conference, and team affinity, there are also disparities based on sport, gender, nationality, and social media. Football is the major revenue-generating sport across most conferences, resulting in the highest number of NIL deals and the highest dollars. According to Opendorse data, the top 3 sports for division 1 NIL compensation are football at 49.6%, men's basketball, at for 18.9%, and women's basketball, at 12.6%. After those three sports, there is a sharp downturn in representation, with the 4th highest being women's volleyball, which account for only 2.5% of deals. Of the remaining 6 sports in the top 10, (softball, baseball, women's track and field, women's gymnastics, men's track and field, and women's swim and dive), none of them have more than 1.9% representation for NIL compensation.

Currently in the state of Arizona it is illegal for High school athletes to monetize their name image or likeness. In fact the Arizona Interscholastic Association (AIA) has gone further to say that any athlete, parent/guardian or anyone acting on behalf of the athlete, getting compensated can result in the suspension and loss of eligibility for that student athlete. Therefore, it would be our recommendation that some state high school do not engage in NIL activity if they are registered members of the AIA. There is a lot of internal pressure for the AIA to change their rulings, however the AIA is trying to hold firm. The reasoning behind the confusion is that it did not get implemented into the collegiate system correctly and it has created a "free agency" system which can be hugely detrimental to the universities. If you were to apply the implications to smaller high schools it would be even worse. Unfortunately, the issue arises as some states are allowing NIL at the High school level, this has led to some students transferring to engage in these activities however this is clearly not an option for every student and could potentially cause issues in the long run (Orbert).

Prior to NIL, a university student athlete played simply for the spirit of their school while the school was cashing in on the use of your name, image and likeness to sell jerseys, tickets and TV contracts. The NCAA was (and still is) generating contracts in the billions.

More confusion occurs because every state has different rules and even each university has different rules regarding the treatment of the athlete as well. While everybody is being very careful not to overstep the bounds of those rules, the rules are constantly changing with little guidance. The issue is that a misstep could make you completely ineligible to play NCAA sports or lose your scholarship.

It is critical that you meet with tax and legal advisors to find out what the laws are in the state where you are going to go to school.

So, what CAN you do? You can now create your own "brand" and convert that to a source of income.

The key to the success of a brand is understanding what your brand represents and if you don't manage it correctly, damage to your brand can prevent you from future opportunities.

Most recently as I write this book Will Smith slapped Chris Rock middle of the Oscar awards. As a result, his brand was damaged. He will now spend time and money repairing his brand in order to be able to restore his image. One of the biggest brands ever built in basketball was Air Jordan. Nike took that brand of one man flying through the air with a ball into billions of dollars.

Becoming a social media "influencer" is one way to generate income, but it comes at a price. In building your brand you also have to decide if you want to be in the public eye. Yes or No? If not, that's a choice, but if you are willing to put in the time, social media may be for you.

Branding is also not just "selling", it can also be related to community service, your brand can be used for social outreach, charity and other community projects.

Chapter 2

WHAT IS NIL

NIL stands for Name Image and Likeness. The NIL change also created many other issues that include recruiting violations incentives for students to go to certain colleges because they can get better NIL deals. Including coaches and boosters touting their ability to create money for the student athletes. It created tax issues relative to state tax and the "Jock Tax" which all professional athletes have been subject to for years and now as a collegiate athlete you may now be subject to the jock tax.

Before that we have to discuss legal terms such as trademarks and copyrights. You own your name, likeness and image, thus nobody else can use it without your authority. It is important that you protect your image with the best legal and tax. In some cases, the colleges are providing education on name image and likeness to give the students some education on how to better manage the money and responsibility what follows.

One key reminder is to watch out for bad contracts. In some early cases, some athletes have been talked into signing a contract for the use of their brand forever. Additionally, in most states, if you are under 18 you now have to determine who can sign a contract in your name. Who can own the company who receives the money? Legally, if you are under 18 you can't legally bind yourself to your contract.

We are going to discuss a little bit about how to legally protect your name, image and likeness. There are two ways of having your brand protected legally and it can be very confusing. I will be using some legal and accounting terms, but they are important. First you need to understand that your "NIL" is what is known as intellectual property 'IP".

You also may have heard terms such as a "Trademark" or "Copyright". For example, the Nike swoosh is a trademark. It is an image only to be used by Nike because everybody who sees that swoosh knows it's representing the Nike brand. Next is the catch phrase "Just Do It". That is a copyright because the words "just" "do" "it" by themselves have no direct correlation to Nike, but combined with the swoosh Nike has secured rights. By filing with the federal government and NIKE is able to protect its rights to that information worldwide.

What is a copyright? A copyright is the rights to words, music, a book, or even software code.

What is a Trademark? A trademark protects the use of a name a product, a slogan or a logo. Most of your NIL work is going to be trademarked.

However, if you are creating original content on TikTok, you are able to copyright that. A movie is protected by copyrights. You can't go out and make Star Wars, because you don't have the rights. Because the two are so different one is handled by the US patent and trademark office while the other is handled by the United States copyright office.

The basic breakdown for understanding what a copyright is starts with some basic building blocks.

Rights creation, tangible medium, duration

Legal Zoom defines Copyright protection as that-which the holder of the work retains exclusive rights to print, display, distribute or perform the work in addition the holder has exclusive rights to publish and transmit the work on the internet.

In order to have the copyright protection it must be an original. Meaning you must be the first one to create this unique item (ex. Song or Movie). That is why Bruno Mars was sued by the family of Marvin Gaye because he used part of one of Marvin Gaye's songs in his own song. As a result, Bruno Mars was legally obligated to pay royalties to the Gaye family.

A copyright must also be fixed in a tangible meeting of expression. Thus it must be in some fixed form such as a book, map, chart, print, sculpture, film, sound recording or computer program. Finally, the duration of a copyright lasts for the life of the author or creator plus 70 years. Most of you are not going to have any copyrighted material as part of your NIL dealings.

Trademarks

Trademarks were started to protect consumers from confusion of looking for goods. Just as the Nike swoosh means Nike to anybody who sees it.

It also ensures sure that you know you are getting a legitimate Nike product. Additionally, the "three lines" on the Adidas means you're getting an Adidas product and not a fake or a copy. For the consumer, it means that if something happens to your Nike shoe you can go back to Nike and say, "hey you guys made a bad shoe".

When trying to secure a trademark you submit your logo to the trademark office. The federal trademark office then does a search to see if there are any similar markings that might cause confusion. If there is not, you own that logo. To do this properly, you may hire a trademark attorney and that means there is a cost. A basic trademark search application might cost $2,500 but can cost more if you need a complicated search or if you were going to try and secure something worldwide.

Chapter 3

CONTRACT AND CONTRACT LAW

Now that NIL deals are being offered at the high school level, the next questions are going to be... How old are you? What are you signing? And What is a contract? Since most high school and some college athletes are not 18, the question becomes, "Can you legally sign a document if you're not 18"?

The answer is that it depends in which state you live, and in which state the contract is written? So, the most important step you need to take (and I will probably reiterate these 50 times in this book) is find a lawyer and an accountant and somebody that needs to understand your specific situation.

Why does the state matter?

For example, if you live in California and are going to play for Georgia. If you are to get a NIL deal from Georgia, the issue is which state has jurisdiction?. Is it California or is it Georgia. California is going to want their money so they are going to look to see if you filed a tax return in the state of California. Georgia is also going to want THEIR money. But we can take this further. If you play for Georgia and you have a game in Alabama, now Alabama wants a share of that income you earned. It is referred to as the "jock tax" and professional athletes file in every state they play a game in and pay taxes in every state as well.

The object of this discussion is not to help you figure it out by reading this book, but to let you know that these issues are out there, and they are real.

There is a case significant IRS case involving race car driver Helio Castroneves who was sued by the United States. He received millions in sponsorship, and because he was sponsored for all of his races worldwide, when he raced United

States, the IRS said that he owed a portion of his sponsorship money, even if he did not win a race, to the USA. The IRS sued him for it, and they won.

This is all very confusing I can imagine, especially for those of you that have never filed a tax return before. You may think it is no big deal because your taxes are not going to be that much. The IRS doesn't necessarily care how much you owe. They are still going to want their money even if it's $1,000 $2,000 or $3,000 or $30,000. What does that mean for you? It means that you have to make sure you've got a good CPA who will help you navigate these complex state and federal tax laws.

So that brings up the Next Question, "What is my Tax and how much is it anyway?"

In general income taxes are based on a bunch of factors including

- Gross income
- Expenses
- State taxes

There are 7 different tax rates that change based on how much you earn. It is very complicated and not worthy of discussing in this book, but you should be aware that your taxes CAN be as much as 50% of your income. Yes, HALF OF YOUR INCOME can go to taxes. So, your question might be, "How do I reduce my taxes?" Taxes are complicated, everchanging and confusing which is why you need a good CPA.

Chapter 4

I Want an LLC

The first question I get asked when we get a now client is "do I need an LLC?" The answer is "maybe". First you must understand what is an LLC and what you can use it for. An LLC can give you an opportunity to save some taxes, but it can also help Create, Expand and Protect your BRAND

Marketing LLC

A marketing LLC is a limited liability company that you can use to manage your endorsement deals, appearance fees, social media accounts, and other income-generating activities from your NIL contracts. A marketing LLC can offer you several advantages, such as:

Liability protection. An LLC is a separate legal entity that shields your personal assets from lawsuits or debts related to your business activities. For example, if someone sues you for breach of contract or defamation, they can only go after the assets of the LLC, not your personal bank accounts or property.

Tax flexibility. An LLC can choose how it wants to be taxed by the IRS. You can elect to be taxed as a sole proprietorship, a partnership, or a corporation. Depending on your income level and expenses, you may be able to save money on taxes by choosing the best option for your situation.

Brand building. An LLC can help you establish and market your personal brand as an athlete and a public figure. You can use your LLC name and logo to create merchandise, websites, podcasts, and other platforms to connect with your fans and sponsors.

Setting up a marketing LLC

WARNING: DO NOT DO THIS YOURSELF, HIRE A PROFEESIONAL

Choose a name for your LLC. The name should be unique, catchy, and related to your brand identity. You also need to make sure that the name is not already taken by another business in your state. You can check the availability of names on the website of the state agency that handles business filings (usually the Secretary of State).

Designate a registered agent. A registered agent is a person or company that agrees to receive legal documents on behalf of your LLC. The registered agent must have a physical address in the state where you form your LLC. You can choose anyone who meets these requirements, including yourself, a friend, a family member, or a professional service company.

File articles of organization. Articles of organization are the official documents that create your LLC with the state. They usually include information such as the name and address of the LLC, the name and address of the registered agent, the purpose and duration of the LLC, and the names of the members (owners) of the LLC. You can file these documents online or by mail with the state agency that handles business filings.

Create an operating agreement. An operating agreement is a document that outlines how your

LLC will be run and how decisions will be made. It can cover topics such as how profits and losses will be distributed, how taxes will be paid, how new members will be admitted or existing members will exit, and how disputes will be resolved. Although an operating agreement is not required by most states, it is highly recommended to have one to avoid potential conflicts and confusion among members.

Get an employer identification number (EIN). An EIN is a unique number assigned by the IRS to identify your LLC for tax purposes. You need an EIN to open a bank account for your LLC, file tax returns, hire employees, and apply for licenses and permits. You can apply for an EIN online for free on the IRS website.

NEXT QUESTION IS – Do I need a Foundation?

In some cases, some clients are choosing to use their NIL for charity, thus building their brand as a community member. This can be done through a Non-Profit Private Foundation

What is a Foundation?

A foundation is a nonprofit organization that gives money away for charitable purposes. A foundation can help you support causes that you care about and make a positive impact in your community and beyond. A foundation can also offer you some benefits, such as:

1. Tax deduction. As a donor to your own foundation, you can deduct up to 30% of your adjusted gross income for cash contributions and up to 20% for appreciated assets (such as stocks or real estate) in the year you make them. You can also carry over any excess deductions for up to five years.

2. Tax exemption. A foundation is exempt-from income tax as long as it follows the IRS rules for 501(c)(3) organizations. However, a foundation may be subject to a 1.39% excise tax on its net investment income. A foundation must also distribute at least 5% of its assets each year for charitable purposes.

3. Control and legacy. As the founder of your own foundation, you can decide how the foundation will be run and who will be in charge of it.

Setting up a Foundation? HIRE A PROFESSIONAL

Choose a name for your foundation. The name should reflect the mission and vision of your foundation and distinguish it from other similar organizations. You also need to make sure that the name is not already taken by another nonprofit in your state. You can check the availability of names on the website of the state agency that handles nonprofit filings (usually the Secretary of State or the Attorney General).

Designate a board of directors. A board of directors is a group of people who oversee the governance and management of your foundation. The board is responsible for setting the policies and goals of the foundation, approving grants and budgets, hiring and evaluating staff, and ensuring compliance with legal and ethical standards. You can choose anyone you trust to serve on your board, such as family members, friends, advisors, or experts in your field of interest. Most states require at least three board members for a nonprofit organization.

File articles of incorporation. Articles of incorporation are the official documents that create your foundation as a nonprofit corporation with the state. They usually include information such as the name and address of the foundation, the name and address of the registered agent, the purpose and duration of the foundation, and the names and addresses of the initial board members. You can file these documents online or by mail with the state agency that handles nonprofit filings.

Apply for tax-exempt status. To qualify as a tax exempt organization under Section 501(c)(3) of the IRS Code, you need to apply to the IRS using Form 1023 or Form 1023-EZ (for smaller organizations). You also need to attach a copy of your articles of incorporation, bylaws, conflict of interest policy, financial statements, and a detailed description of your charitable activities and grantmaking procedures. The IRS will review your application and determine if your foundation meets the requirements for tax exemption.

Create bylaws and policies. Bylaws are a document that outlines how your foundation will be governed and operated. They can cover topics such as the roles and responsibilities of board members and officers, how board meetings will be conducted, how committees will be formed, how grants will be awarded, how conflicts of interest will be handled, and how bylaws can be amended. Policies are documents that provide guidance on specific issues or situations that may arise in your foundation's work. Some common policies for foundations are grantmaking policy, investment policy, spending policy, whistle-blower policy, document retention policy, and gift acceptance policy.

NEW 2024 Corporate Transparency Act

Reporting the Beneficial Owner of your LLC

IMPORTANT NEW LAW EFFECTIVE JANUARY 1, 2024

What is the CTA tax law?

The CTA directs the U.S. Department of the Treasury's Financial Crimes Enforcement Network ("FinCEN") to propose rules requiring certain types of entities to file a report identifying each entity's beneficial owners as well as the natural persons who formed the entity, unless an exemption applies

The CTA aims to combat illicit activity including tax fraud, money laundering, and financing for terrorism by capturing more ownership information for specific U.S. businesses operating in or accessing the country's market

Starting in 2024, the Corporate Transparency Act ("CTA") mandates certain entities (primarily small and medium-size businesses) created in or registered to do business in the United States report information about their beneficial owners—the individuals who ultimately own or control a company—to the Financial Crimes Enforcement Network ("FinCEN").

Currently, as the law stands, some State Board of Accountancys (our governing body) has established that the CTA is considered to be the "Practice of Law" and as such some CPA's are not allowed to prepare and file the Beneficial Owner Reports. Because all CPA's are not permitted to render any legal services, you will need to contact an attorney regarding the legal or regulatory aspects of your LLC to maintain compliance with the CTA

I strongly encourage that you consult with qualified legal counsel experienced in this area if there is any question regarding the Beneficial Ownership of your LLC. The penalties for ignoring this rule are 10,000.00 and up to 2 years in Jail.

We talked about your "team" of advisors. This is another reason you need to have a trusted advisory team keeping you out of jail.

Chapter 5

BUILDING YOUR TEAM

The first thing I tell potential professional athlete clients is that I am your "NO" person. I tell them that if they don't want to say "no" to someone, have them call me and I will say "NO" for you. Also, I am straight with my clients. If I don't like an idea, a decision, an option or suggestion I will say "no." Many advisors, as Profit says in an article from Forbes.com, are scared to say "no." As an athlete I ask that you respect that opinion when your advisor says "no." You do have a right to know why, but understand that their advice reflects years of professional experience and education. Listen to them, then you can make an informed and intelligent decision. I tell advisors who want to work with athletes two things: 1) don't be afraid to say "no" and 2) remember that it's their money and our job is to help them manage it.

Great advisors can be compared to "life coaches" because they can help you manage some of the complex financial decisions throughout your life such as buying a car, house, or saving for college. We deal with these decisions on a daily basis. In my career, I have negotiated the purchase of Ferraris, Bentleys, Range Rovers, McLarens, Porsches, Aston Martins as well as Fords Jeeps and Chevys. Great advisors will help you reach your lifelong financial and personal goals.

When you are in the process of choosing your professional advisory team, it is important that you evaluate that team according to the advice and support they will give you when you are done playing. Most of the time, the remaining advisors are your investment advisor, your attorney (for estate planning and business), and your CPA. These are the ones who will help you transition to the next part of your life.

Working with your investment team both while you are playing and after you retire is important. Part of "working" with your team means understanding what they do, what recommendations they are making and more importantly WHY they are making those recommendations. Many young athletes that have received a large amount of money from a signing bonus or large salaries have said to me that they feel "dumb" asking questions. There is a misconception that RICH PEOPLE ARE SMART. While many wealthy individuals are smart, most of them have accumulated that education over years of working with professionals, trial and error as well as additional schooling. At 22 years old there is not an expectation that you should know everything just because you have money. Be aware that it is okay indeed to ask questions. IT IS YOUR MONEY and do not forget that.

Ask those Questions

Above all, don't be afraid to ask a question because you fear it may make you look dumb. I am a CPA, and I specialize in taxes. I have clients who are doctors who are highly educated and perform major operations such as heart transplants or brain surgery. Yet they know nothing about taxes and business. Taxes are not their specialty. If they ask a question about their taxes, it doesn't mean they're dumb. It only means they have not been educated in that field. Taxes are not your specialty. Your athletic abilities are. If you ask questions about your finances or taxes, it doesn't mean you're dumb. Always ask. Always keep informed.

The most important thing in choosing an advisor is to find someone with whom you can connect with and build trust. By having more than one advisor you will have "another set of eyes" looking at your accounts.

In my first book I discussed your team of advisors for Legal, Finance and Taxes. It's time to cover a little more about attorneys and their specialties. Be aware you may need more than one lawyer because you may need legal advice and representation for various things. For instance, for creating wills and passing along your assets to your heirs, you would need an estate planning attorney. If you have bought a franchise or have started your own business, you may need a business attorney to help with possible business problems or help you set up a corporation. Maybe a legal issue with your taxes might arise in which your CPA could not help. Then you would need a tax attorney. Maybe you want to sue someone, or perhaps you're being sued. You would need a litigating attorney or a defense attorney for those situations. You can use different lawyers for different purposes, depending upon your legal needs.

For your financial bookkeeping and tax preparation, I recommend a Certified Public Accountant or accounting firm as your best resource. Although regulations are a little different in each state, Certified Public Accountants must have over one-hundred and fifty hours of college-level accounting classes, must pass a six-part test (which can take 2 ½ days) as well as maintaining their licenses with forty hours of continuing education every year. CPAs are constantly improving their skills and being educated on changing tax laws. Many CPA's, like my firm, also offer business management services. Our firm not only deals with taxes, we also provide services and advice regarding business financing, business structure, large asset purchases like homes and autos, personal financial management, and other day-to-day finances. I said earlier that you, as a professional athlete, operate like a small business; thus, the CPA acts as your CFO (Chief Financial Officer) managing your day-to-day business affairs as they are integrated into your long term and more advanced financial affairs.

An investment advisor is also part of your Triad of Advisors I would like to speak more about financial advisors because they are part of your continuing support group after you finishplaying. Just like accountants become certified, so do financial advisors. Just as you want to have a Certified Public Accountant on your support team, you also want to have a Certified Financial Planner (CFP). CFPs have licenses to sell or invest in stocks, bonds, or insurance. There are different types of licenses for financial planners, and becoming certified is not easy.

It takes two years for a financial planner to become certified. Prerequisites for certification include a bachelor's degree and three years of experience as a financial planner. A Certified Financial Planner could hold several types of licenses.

- Securities License – This license allows the CFP to sell mutual funds, life insurance, and investment trusts.   To hold this license, the CFP must be able to manage all aspects of accounts and purchasing.
- Securities Agent – This license allows the CFP to purchase or sell mutual funds, stocks, or bonds.
- Uniform Investment License – This license allows the CFP to be an investment advisor.
- General Securities Representative – This license allows the CFP to be qualified to advise and answer information concerning

general securities such as stocks, bonds, and investments.

The above is a very broad and general overview of different licenses a CFP may have and training a CFP must undergo. There are additional licenses a financial planner can obtain, such as a Series 65, Series 6 or Series 7, all of which allow them to sell different types of investments. It is enough to say that a financial planner must undergo detailed testing before he or she can become certified. Just as a Certified Public Accountant is the highest in his or her field, so is a Certified Financial Planner the highest in the financial planning field.

A financial advisor or financial planner protects, handles, and grows your financial assets. That person's job is to assist with your selection of investments to fit your goals as well as your risk tolerance levels. While you're actively playing and earning money, you may have a high-risk tolerance because you have a steady income. As you get older, accumulate more wealth or retire, your risk tolerance may change. Depending upon where you are in your life, you may have different investment goals and financial plans. To be certain those goals and plans are met, you need a Certified Financial Planner to explain your investments and to manage them. It is the CFP's job to help you understand your investments and how they are performing on an ongoing basis. It is his or her job to help you invest as wisely as you can, so your financial needs are always met.

The US Securities and Exchange Commission (the SEC) www.sec.gov has fantastic information on investing and choosing a broker. Some of their advice is as follows and is worth repeating.

First, THINK through your financial objectives. This is where we talked about having goals and a plan.

Before you hire anyone:

- Talk and Meet with several firms. As we mentioned earlier, Kareem Abdul-Jabar lost investments because he simply went with the recommendation of other teammates.
- Perform a FINRA Broker Check, as we discussed earlier, to verify history of any past disciplinary actions.
- Understand HOW they will get paid. Is it commissions? Is it a percentage of assets under their management? Are there any additional fees?

- Find out if they are a member of Securities Investor Protection Corporation (SIPC), which provides limited protection if the broker becomes insolvent.

When opening an account there are still more questions to ask, including:

- Who will control the decision making on your account? Does the broker have the ability to make trades with our without your consent?
- Is there a provision to go "on margin" or borrow against your current investments for new investments? Going "on margin" means you are borrowing money to buy investments, which can be dangerous and has caused many wealthy investors to lose everything when the market declines.
- Never invest in a product you do not FULLY understand, and if you don't, get a second opinion from a CPA or another advisor.

Be Alert for:

- Recommendations based on "inside or confidential information", it's called INSIDER TRADING and it means GOING TO JAIL.
- Suspicious representations of spectacular profits, such as your money will "double in six months."
- Guarantees that you will NOT lose money or agreements that the broker will share in losses on your account.
- Watch for too many transactions in your account (also known as "churning").
- Any assurance that any error in your account is because of "computer or clerical error."

Always Looking Forward

There will come a time when the athlete part of your life is over. One of the challenges for any former athlete is the loss of your support. While you were playing you had coaches, teammates, your agent as well as perhaps a Public Relations firm, and the administration of the team or college. Suddenly, that support disappears. It will happen and it will happen quickly. As you are no longer part of a "team" you will have feelings of being alone with nowhere to go.

NOW, while you are still in the game, is the time to begin looking ahead to your transition from being an active-athlete to being a former-athlete As you prepare for your future of "civilian life," it is important to understand that you will continue to need a professional support team, your "three-legged stool professional team," that you now have. The support team you have now may not be the same ones you will need moving to your post-athletic career. You may need different areas of expertise to support you as you transition. Your transition does not have to be one of anxiety or dread. It can and should be one of excitement and anticipation as you move to remake yourself bolstered by a solid support team.

Follow up to Choosing your Advisor: Separation of Duties

As a CPA we are taught to develop internal controls in a business to minimize the likelihood of fraud. One of those first aspects of internal control is the separation of duties. That means that no single person does everything. For instance, the person that collects the money does not reconcile the bank statements. By instituting separation of duties in any business, you minimize the likelihood of fraud. While you can never completely eliminate fraud, it is a risk you can minimize.

When a player comes to me and says "oh my agent handles everything" or "my financial advisor handles everything" I always stop and take a breath and try to explain the dangers of such arrangements.

While having one person or one company handling every aspect of your personal and business life does not necessarily mean that you will be defrauded, or that you will lose money; it increases the likelihood of that happening. That is why I always explain the importance of having those three professionals operating as separate advisors, while still working together.

You must remember that as an athlete people will always tell you "you're the quarterback" in the NFL or that "you're the manager" in baseball or they will remind you that "you're the captain of the team". However, you are actually the OWNER of the entire team. It is all your money, and that's very important for you to remember. You are the one that hires and fires the coach, hires and fires the manager, hires and fires the offensive coordinator, hires and fires the pitching coach, or the batting coach. Everybody works FOR you.

I do not want to scare anyone into thinking that just because one person is doing everything that fraud will occur. While there are some fantastic organizations that have such broad knowledge that they actually can do everything and do it well, many others promise that service, but fail miserably. The main problem is that you are most likely not educated enough in taxes, law and investments to know if they are taking the correct action or not.

It's critical to ensure that your three advisors, your agent/attorney, your investment advisor, and your CPA are working together. While they should be collaborating for your best interest, they will also watch out for you individually to make sure that you are getting the best advice.

Many times, I will call an agent and say "hey, we have an issue with our client", or I will call the investment advisor to work on end of year tax planning ideas. In my experience the most overlooked member of your team is the CPA, not because I am a CPA, but because as a CPA I bring a different level of knowledge that an agent or investment advisor may not possess.

I had an investment advisor tell me that they did not want to take any deductions because they were afraid of the IRS. What that indicates is that the advisor did not understand tax law, and did not understand working with the IRS. Their firm has either had a bad experience or absolutely no experience with an IRS audit and a capable CPA. There are two things that we say in our profession. First, "Pigs get fed" and secondly, "hogs get slaughtered, don't be a pig".

In addition, famous Judge Learned Hand once stated regarding Income taxes, "Anyone may arrange his affairs so that his taxes shall be as low as possible; he is not bound to choose that pattern which best pays the treasury. There is not even a patriotic duty to increase one's taxes or public duty to pay more than the law demands." -Judge Learned Hand, Helvering v. Gregory, 69 F.2d 809, 810 (2d Cir. 1934), aff'd, 293 U.S. 465 (1935)

When you start picking your team, make sure you pick a team that you think will work together and be able to act independently from one another. Make sure that if you want to terminate one of the three, that it won't affect your relationship with the other two. Make sure that if one of the three is not acting in your best interest, the other two will let you know. It is unfortunate that you have to create this system of checks and balances, but not having knowledge of the law, investments or taxation, you cannot possibly know if the answers you are getting are in your best interest.

Takeaways, Questions and Actions:

1. Find at least one CPA – Talk to them.
2. Find at least one Attorney – Talk to them.
3. Find at least one Investment Advisor – Talk to them.

Chapter 6

WORKING WITH YOUR TEAM

Consider a four-legged table and a three-legged stool. If one leg is removed from the table, that table is able to still stand, albeit a bit wobbly. However, if one leg is removed from the three-legged stool, the stool falls, as it must have all three legs to remain upright.

The same can be said in small business and is an absolute for any athlete. There are three "legs," that we will call The Professionals, which are critical to your professional structure to "remaining upright." Those three professionals are an attorney, investment advisor, and Certified Public Accountant.

You depend upon an attorney to deliver legal protection and advice. A common term used by everyone is "estate planning," which is a prime example of the importance of an attorney's services. The late Aretha Franklin died without preparing a will. Because of this oversight, approximately $30 million will be taken from her estimated $80 million estate. A personal attorney is desirable for all legal matters one may encounter.

The second professional key to off the field and long-term financial success is your investment advisor. Commonly they will have initials such as CFP or CLU. There are over 190 different "professional designations" which can be found at https://www.finra.org/investors/professional-designations. A prudent person depends upon a financial consultant to protect, maintain and grow the value of financial assets. The vehicles used to accomplish this may be life insurance, stocks, bonds, mutual funds, or annuities. It is critical that your investment advisor knows your short and long-term financial goals. A wise professional athlete makes certain a reputable financial consultant is providing sound financial advice and asset supervision to maintain the athletes' monetary health.

The third professional is a Certified Public Accountant. Your business asset is your talent and most professional athlete's finances act like small businesses. Indispensable to you will be your CPA/business manager who will watch and manage your business and personal affairs from tax planning and return preparation to crucial business consultation. Many public tax preparers are IRS authorized, but do not understand the complex tax situations that plague professional athletes, and many times will cause potential problems with the IRS. Having a CPA Certification is a key qualification for proper tax planning advice.

The same way the three legs are critical to support the stool, professional athletes need three strong supportive professionals to successfully support their business lives. Without strong Legal, Investment, and financial professionals, the athlete can risk being open to the common and public problems of fraud, misrepresentation, IRS Tax liens and possible jail time for errors of judgment.

Similar to the fact that all three legs must be in working order and that all members of the "coaching team" work together, it is imperative your professional advisor's function together in your best interest. Teamwork is vital. You know full well the absolute necessity of teamwork on a playing field, a basketball court, or crammed in a bobsled. Just as selecting a coaching team, it is absolutely critical that you carefully choose the business team. Periodic team meetings in which all professionals and you gather to discuss the common "game plan" are excellent in keeping everyone involved on the same page, running the same direction on the same track, and planning the same game.

Planning? Yes! Game plans are essential to any sport. Financial plans are fundamental to any successful business. The question arises, "What is a plan?" A dictionary definition is "a system for achieving an objective; a method of doing something that is worked out in advance." Most certainly, that definition describes game plans which are systems for achieving objectives of winning games. Professional athletes are intimately familiar with and understand game plans; but what about financial or business plans? Sometimes, not so much.

Understanding both game and business plans is crucial for your future success. Such success results from a clear vision of anticipated goals. You must begin your journey into and out of your sport with clear goals in mind. All your actions with your professional team should be in line with the achievement of those goals. Meetings with your team are critical as you will be able to meet and discuss and alter your goals and objectives to meet the changing environment.

However, just as you do during a game, you must be flexible and work in an ever-changing landscape. Injuries, transfers, economic issues, as well as family life events and a multitude of other issues will create needed changes in your goals. At that point everything changes instantly and now you will be going to "Plan B."

What then? What of your plan? What about your Team? Is it still needed?

Unequivocally the answer is yes! You, professional athlete or not, need knowledge of legal matters such as living wills, investments in instruments such as 401Ks, and tax topics such as withholdings and refunds. For this knowledge you still need the support of experienced professionals I've mentioned: an attorney, an investment counselor, and a CPA. Building a personal relationship with these team members, as well as creating team rapport among all, becomes vitally important for the long run.

It takes a well-oiled machine, a closely working team to create a successful Game Plan. Your continued success towards your goals will depend upon skillful, superior, and trustworthy teamwork.

Success. According to the dictionary, "success" is several things. It is an "achievement of intention," "something that turns out well," or an "attainment of fame, wealth, or power." Normally, success is wonderful when an intention is achieved, or something turns out for the good. Attainment of fame, wealth, or power is a positive accomplishment as well. You're on the field, success breeds confidence in realizing intended athletic goals. It also can create a false confidence that success ON the field will spill over to success OFF the field. Highly successful athletes are vulnerable to pitfalls off the fields without the proper level of advice and a strong support team.

You should be aware of these similar feelings of invincibility. The ability and confidence for a boxer to step into the ring can be an asset or a detriment outside of the ring. But as we discussed previously, while you're ON the field accomplishments take a team of trainers, coaches and teammates, your OFF the field success also requires a strong team of professionals. Success may be short lived, a solid advisory team is not. Whether highly successful, somewhat successful or moderately successful, YOU will always triumph with such a team supporting your goals and objectives as they align with a healthy, productive business and life plan.

Confidence. Confidence exhibits deep strength, poise, and sureness. Confidence is modest. Confidence drives success. A person can be assuredly confident in their athletic accomplishments and an ego driven by assured self-confidence is one which delivers top achievements in sports performance, performing arts, or any profession. A highly successful athlete is one who has bedrock self-confidence in their abilities to positively perform functions of their particular sport and attain its highest objectives. You have the confidence necessary to perform at the highest level of your sport. But it is critical that you realize and truly understand that your capabilities ON the field may not translate into the same abilities and success OFF the field.

The important point to remember is that having experienced coaches greatly aid in navigating the changing landscape of life during and after the game. Some challenges are fundamental life issues, and others are a complex matter of business, legal and investment decisions. We hope that you recognize the value of such guides, mentors, or experienced advisers and counselors.

Certainly, one's attorney, investment counselor, and CPA are experienced advisers and indispensable to one's support. They are essential foundations upon which a professional athlete's business management lies.

A Mentor

In addition to the three professional advisors, it is important that you find a Mentor. What is a Mentor? Where does one find a mentor? Who is a mentor? The Dictionary defines a mentor as an experienced and trusted adviser. The knowledge, advice, and resources of a mentor depends on how you develop and build your relationship with your mentor relationship. Your mentoring relationship is personal and unique to you. A mentor may share information with you about his or her own career path, as well as provide guidance, motivation, emotional support.

How to find a Mentor? A mentor may be your family member, your father/mother, your aunt/ uncle or Sister/brother, it may also be a pastor or rabbi, a professor or coach, but it may also be someone you have not met yet. Networking is valuable in finding and building a relationship with a potential mentor. I will discuss more about networking later in this book, but it is important that you realize your brand value as an athlete and how to use it to your advantage, to reach your goals. An easy start is as simple as attending functions of your university. Charity events that are sponsored by the university or boosters are easy ways to meet local business leaders. Professional association networking is particularly helpful in building portfolios of connections for professional athletes. Often athletes find mentors in coaches, trainers, owners, or family.

To recap, I hope that by reading this book you will begin to develop your own "game plan" that you, an established or soon-to-be successful professional, will recognize and appreciate that you cannot "go it alone" in negotiating pitfalls, potholes, and problems that will undoubtedly occur in your profession and personal life. Positive and profitable outcomes for both are significantly influenced by and greatly depend upon professional and personal support systems. As you prepare and follow game plans for participating in your sport, so should you prepare and follow the game plans for your business and life affairs. Using your three-professional team of an attorney, an investment advisor, and a CPA as well as developing a relationship with your mentor, you can successfully achieve your goals.

Takeaway Questions and Notes:

1. Post Career – what do I want to do?

2. Make a list of Whom do I know TODAY that can help me TOMORROW.

3. What do you think are your hurdles that will slow you down.

4. If I won the lottery, what would I do?

Chapter 7

Networking and Branding

Networking, it's not what you know...In her book Fit for Business, Taylor Pak states that when she was recruited for college soccer, "you have limited time to show a coach who you are and what potential you have." "Trying to master your elevator speech at the age of 16 is difficult." However, she realized that the experience helped and guided her in realizing that she had already had many "job interviews."

"It's fair to say that the recruiting process is equitable to the job search, which means that student athletes already have a great deal of practice. Finding the right home for your unique personality and skill set is not an easy task. It takes research (again lots of research) and some time to figure out what your strengths and weaknesses are."

As an athlete, you already have the tools and experience of the job interview. Taylor states that "it's OK to feel uncertainty and discomfort while thinking about the next chapter of your life because you have the OPPORTUNITY to make something of yourself."

There's an old saying in business that "it's not what you know but who you know," which holds very true in today's business environment.

Networking can make a huge difference in finding your post- athletic opportunities. Succeed or fail, it may also make the difference between surviving the three-year transition out of athletics or not; the difference of finding the job or position that you want or not. In interviews with my clients, who are former professional athletes, every one of them will tell me that it's very difficult to transition out of athletics.

My experience is that it takes approximately three years to make that transition. Some may be shorter, and some may be longer. I use the term athletics and not PROFESSIONAL athletics as there are struggles in both the post collegiate world (called "post-graduate depression") as well as transition from professional athletics. The issue being that you are no longer identified as an athlete. A student athlete at the age of 20, you have been playing your sport for perhaps over 15 years, 75% of your life, and probably 100% of what you can remember.

You may be able to transition out of athletics when you complete college, straight into a job. You may be able to transition out of athletics after playing professional sports for 10 years as well, but there is still a transition period when you are no longer on a team mandated schedule where you are being told where, what and when. You are now completely on your own. It is very difficult when the time ends as an athlete. As a collegiate athlete, you are no longer on a schedule being told when to eat, sleep, study, practice, play, be there, and be here. In addition to the scheduled life you are used to, there is one more big change when you transition out of the professional world, MONEY.

There comes a time in EVERY professional athlete's life when the money stops and your support group, the people that you've been around for years, are no longer there. Your attorney will still be involved with your changing planning and estate planning needs, your CPA will still be involved with your business and your taxes. However, many of your now former teammates may be having their own issues or maybe they're still playing, and you are no longer part of that club.

Now what do I do?

When that moment hits, and you realize that you are no longer a collegiate or professional athlete that is when all your prior NETWORKING efforts come into play. I cannot stress the importance of networking. What is networking? Networking is connecting with other people in business, industries or professions that are of interest to you. It also involves meeting people who might be able to help you in the future. When I talked about "it's not what you know but who you know," that is the key to networking.

Harvey MacKay, a well-known syndicated columnist, author and business networking guru, talks about knowing your clients and how critical that knowledge is to be able to grow and maintain a business. It's the same way for a student athlete or a professional athlete, with one exception. As an athlete, you may have the ability to get your "foot in the door" where others cannot. For instance, as a member of a collegiate athletic team, you have an opportunity to interact with alumni and boosters, all of whom may be successful businesses people in the community. When attending charity events, it's important that you "kick butt and take names." More importantly, keep the information of whom you met. You may want to have somebody help you follow up after meetings through email, calling or setting up a lunch. Meeting those contacts can be beneficial, especially if they can help you with a project or a business in which you are interested in. Take advantage of the opportunities presented to you.

Wayne Kimmel, in his book "Six Degrees of Wayne Kimmel," the networking guru and venture capitalist at Seventy-Six Capital has "the Gospel" for networking.

> How do you meet the people that will become your most trusted and influential relationships? You have to go out and find them. You never know who (sic) they're going to be, so you have to cast as wide a net as possible."

Networking as a student athlete is becoming similar to that of a professional athlete. There are more opportunities for you to get out into the community and meet the people that are going to help you when you are an ex-athlete or former player.

There are two things to remember in networking. First, the "never say no" attitude. Kareem Abdul Jabbar gave the advice to get out there and "engage?" While you don't want to overdo your schedule, you never know what new opportunities will come from attending an event. The other is "don't worry about what people want," instead flip it and look at it as "what can THEY do for you." Many times, you do not realize that you have the power to meet anyone. I am sure that if LeBron James wanted to meet the president of any fortune 100 company, Microsoft, Uber, Amazon it would only take one phone call. While you may not be LeBron, you still have a great opportunity to meet people in your community. If you attend a smaller university or a large university in a small town there are still opportunities to meet with local business leaders and talk with you about what you want to do in the future.

Create your contact list, what used to be known as a Rolodex. While many of you are being taught how to use LinkedIn, note that, unlike Instagram, it is not a goal to have a million connections. Instead, you want to try and make your contacts fewer but more important. Quality vs Quantity. You are better off knowing 20 people really well than having over 500 contacts that you barely know.

Examples of the two ideas from above are from two former Arizona Cardinals players. First, John Bronson tells the story of his "never say no" experience. Once one of his teammates called him to say he wasn't able to go the (then called) Phoenix Open golf tournament and wanted to know if John would fill in for him. "Sure," he said without knowing exactly what he was doing. As it turned out, John was going to be a "celebrity" caddy for the Pro-AM. John spent the next 8 hours a celebrity caddy and ended up spending 8 hours talking to Jimmy Walker. Mr. Walker is a local, well-known and very well-connected investment advisor. Mr. Walker happens to also host a very significant charity event for the Mohammed Ali Foundation for Parkinson's Disease. The event is called "Fight Night," and it's a high-ranking social event. He invited John to attend. John said he went to the event feeling like "a big man in town" because he was an Arizona Cardinals player and was invited to this major event. He was a celebrity. When he walked in, however, he found himself in the middle of A-listers from Hollywood, politics, and business. It was at this event that John will tell you that he met his best friend and long-time mentor and business advisor. Never say no.

John Skelton, another former Arizona Cardinals player, had a different lesson. In preparing this book, I asked him, "What are the things that you wished you would have done when you were playing?" He said that as an athlete he was always cautious when at an event. He was wary of what people wanted FROM him. Because, as an athlete, you are trained to be wary of people taking advantage of you, he said would put up a wall to guard against that risk. In hindsight, he said he wished would have approached the events completely differently, with the view of "what can YOU do for ME." He now realizes that he could have received valuable contacts in the business world if he had been open to networking with people instead of closing them off. All of this "connecting" does not mean that you should be open to everyone without properly vetting a new contact; you should always make sure to have a member of your trusted advisory team to help you do that. You might even perhaps take a "wingman" that can help you "work the room."

Much like in the dating world and being at a party, everyone at the event knows why they are there. It may be drinks or cigars at a bar or restaurant; playing golf; attending a charity event or sometimes just being open to new contacts when you are doing your normal day-to-day activities. All colleges and sports teams sponsor charity events that you may, as a member of the team, be required to attend.

Community and business leaders are most of the attendees at these events and it's a great opportunity for you to meet people who might be able to help you transition from your "sporting world" to the "regular world" when that time comes. I urge you to get comfortable and be open to every opportunity you have and build your network of meaningful contacts.

Your meaningful contacts are people you know something about. They are not just a connection you made by clicking "Accept." You may know about their jobs, what they actually do, their birthdays or family members; you may have some common business acquaintances. The longer you are in business, the more you network, the more your contacts may become your friends as well.

A good example of this is a business networking event I attended. At the meeting there was an Arizona Cardinal's Player, who was on injured reserve. He was sitting with the other Cardinals players and not meeting with the business people who also attended the event. I mentioned to him, "You realize that everybody in this room is afraid to come up and talk to you?" He said, "What do you mean?" I told him, "I understand you're on injured reserve, but you play in the NFL. You realize that everybody in this room would love to just chat with you. You have an opportunity to meet all these business people. Take advantage of it."

Every chance you have, get the contact information. Show interest in what they're about. Do not be surprised, but they will be far more interested in YOUR stories of being an athlete. Build your networking file. Follow up with people you've met. Go to events. Develop real friendships with people outside of your athletic world. Grow your support system. As a professional athlete, you have a wonderful opportunity to network.

More gospel from Wayne: "there will be nights when you would rather hangout with your family and friends instead of going to a networking, political or charity event. GO ANYWAY. You never know who you will meet. This is a long game. Building relationships is like a marathon, not a sprint."

Building Brand Value

In addition to growing your post career portfolio, it is important that you show who you are TODAY. Who are you and what your BRAND is.

First, what is branding? Simply put, in the retail world, a brand is something that identifies a product or an idea in people's minds. For example, "Kleenex" conjures up a small paper tissue in people's minds whether or not that tissue is a Kleenex brand tissue, Puff, or Angel Soft. If you sneezed, you probably would say to me, "Hand me a Kleenex, please." I doubt if you would ask me to hand you a facial tissue. Other common, successful retail brands include Saran Wrap and Band Aids and hundreds of other household names.

Athlete Brand Life

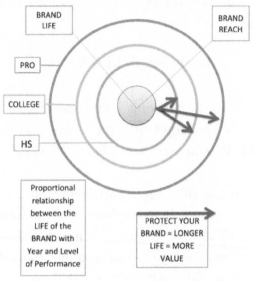

Athlete Brand Life Circle

The figure above can illustrate Brand Life for the athlete. Brand life or Brand Value have both a geographical (local, state, national or international) reach as well as a time-life to it.

A name like "Michael Jordan" has a brand value that has a worldwide geographic reach and probably has a brand life value that will last for quite some time. While you might not be Michael Jordan, Wayne Gretzky, Joe Montana or Derek Jeter, you do have Brand Value if you play professional sports, and in some cases if you have brand value if you play Collegiate Sports (otherwise you might not be getting a scholarship.)

When you are involved in NCAA athletics, you have an automatic brand by just being part of the team. You are an ASU Sun Devil, UCLA Bruin, Clemson Tiger etc. Use that to your advantage. Additionally, you have the ability to build that brand value while you are playing so that it has longevity and prominence after you retire from sports.

Branding and Philanthropy

One of the most common ways an athlete can create a brand is through charitable work. Because, when we talk about media misconceptions, we discuss that the GOOD stories can gain media attention and build brand value. College and professional teams are always involved in the community. You have a jump start and are probably already doing some work within the community through your team. Successful athletes can bring a strong brand value and influence to a charity, thereby securing the brand value of the athlete. Having your name and likeness out in the community can be one of the strongest assets you bring to an employer, team, college or endorsement sponsor. As we talk about your name and likeness, let's try to look at what a BRAND is and how you can create, grow, maintain and monetize your BRAND.

You can have a brand that represents you off the court and a separate one that represents you on the court. While your "on the field" brand is really based on how you play the game, your "off the field" brand is based on your outside activities, community involvement, being a voice of the team or your sport, and even how you represent yourself online.

Basically, your brand is how people see you, hear you, your mission, your value, and your image. WHY DO I CARE how people see me? Well, if you have aspirations to create income with some OFF the field opportunities, YOU SHOULD CARE. For example, what kind of "brand" do you think of when you think of Larry Fitzgerald? You "know" them by their brands.

UNFORTUNATELY, in today's world, what you portray to people is how others see you. Don't forget by "others" I mean to include future Coaches, General Managers, Employers as well as the general public. Perception is reality. You create your own brand in their minds, and that is how you can FAIL or SUCCEED in creating a brand. Now you might read this and say, "I don't care." And that's OK. You do NOT have to create a brand, market a brand and monetize a brand. This chapter may not be relevant to you.

However, whether you like it or not, you are being judged by the impression you leave on others and the impression you make on social media. When a prospective College, Professional Team or other Employer looks at you as a candidate, they currently have staff that will search social media to see if there is ANY dirt on you. Trust me, I do the same when I look to hire a new staff member.

This is especially true with social media! If you portray yourself as a wild partygoer on Instagram, people may see you as immature and irresponsible. If they see you attending charity events, they may see you as a responsible community leader. Whatever image you put out on social media can, for better or worse, become your brand. You want to be extremely careful how you brand yourself on social media because once you put something on the Web it never goes away.

Which of those items from your past would you want shown to the public, your potential team coach/GM or to your possible employer? Whatever you put on social media, you put on your resume. However you portray yourself on Social Media is how you build your brand. Build your brand thoughtfully. Build your brand carefully. Build your brand effectively for the best results for you.

You can use social media to your advantage to develop a mature, reliable, and sensible brand for yourself, or you can irresponsibly create a foolish, immature, and unreliable brand. You can use social media to build your brand as a dependable and levelheaded person or you can damage your future. It's up to you. What type of person do you want people to see you as? How do you want to be branded?

Networking and Branding. They go hand-in-hand. As you network with people, you also build your brand in their eyes. Whether you're networking in person with others at a social event or sitting at a computer posting on social media, you're building your brand. Step outside of yourself and look at you through other people's eyes. What do they see at a business meeting or social gathering? What kind of impression do they get about you from your Instagram posts or Twitter feed? The answers to those questions are up to you. You are the writer of your life's story. You are the builder of your brand. Get out there and network! With every hand you shake and with every post you post, build your fine, strong, outstanding brand!

- Networking Tips
  - Get out there
  - Follow Up
  - Don't be shy
  - Get Help

- Branding Ideas, developing your own personal mission statement
  - Find your own identity
  - What do you stand for?
  - Mind your Mission Statement
  - Donor Advised Funds are an easy way to Create Brand

Takeaways and questions:

1. What is my brand on the field?

2. What do I want my brand to be off the field?

3. Who can help me network if I am uncomfortable?

4. List 3 events I can attend.

5. List 3 business contacts I know and can reach out to.

6. List 3 business contacts I WANT to talk to and who can help me connect.

Chapter 8

MONEY AND BANKING

Two interconnected financial errors that can drastically affect your money are overspending and falling into debt. In the game, athletes face certain risks on the field — for example, the possibility of getting injured during a game, or facing penalties for illegal plays. (VISA Financial Soccer)

Yet, simple actions like warming up before hitting the field and knowing the rules of the game can help minimize the possibility of either scenario. Likewise, certain actions and oversights can negatively impact your personal finances. For example, adopting bad habits like buying items on credit that you can't really afford and failing to create a budget can lead easily to accumulating unwanted debt. Living beyond your means and buying more WANTS than you can afford, impulse buying, and other bad habits can, in the long run, destroy your financial wellbeing.

Debt is when you owe money. Debt is not a bad thing, but you have to be careful not to accumulate more than you can afford to pay back. One way to get into debt is to make impulsive spending decisions without considering whether or not you can afford or really need something.

In this chapter I want to talk about money. There is a common saying that "Money makes the world go 'round." Money is what we want more of when we work; it allows us to pay for stuff; pay for food, do charitable work, have fun.

Plain and simple, let's be honest, we all want to obtain enough wealth to accomplish our goals and dreams, but we also want to spend it wisely. Since you probably don't walk around with all of your cash in a duffel bag like Floyd Mayweather, it's important that you understand what money really is and how it works?

Money and banking are almost inseparable. Issues with money and banking can be complicated, and that is why you need the three professional financial advisors on your team. Simply, what is money? It is a medium of legal exchange used to measure the value of goods and services. In today's world money consists of gold, silver, or coins and paper. In ancient Rome salt was used as money. The Roman government paid their army and government workers with measures of salt because salt was an extremely valuable commodity then. In fact, our word "salary" stems from the Roman word "salarium," meaning "salt money."

What happens to money when you earn it? If you are smart, you put it in a bank. Thus, it's very important that you understand your relationship with your bank.

A bank is defined as "a business that keeps money for individual people or companies, exchanges currencies, makes loans, and offers other financial services." It's easy to think that you merely deposit your money in your bank, and it sits there for you to withdraw it when you need it. That is not the way banks work. The primary function of any bank is to use money deposited by you and others to lend out for other people to buy real estate, start and grow businesses, improve homes, buy cars, or pay for college tuition, just to name a few. When you deposit your money, it goes into a big pool of money with all the other customers making deposits.

The Bank may give you 1% or 2% interest on your money. Meanwhile, they take that money, and they loan it out to somebody else to buy a house, a car or even to start a business. On that loan they charge them a larger interest rate and the bank makes money based on the difference between the two interest rates. Example: they may pay you 2% and they may charge somebody else 8%; they use that 6% difference to run the bank and make a profit.

Banks move money into the economy by making loans and being paid back with interest. Part of your money, along with other depositors' money, is always moving through society and helping the economy.

Since you don't carry around your cash in a bag, you can have access to your cash through an ATM going to the bank or just using a credit or debit card to spend the money that you have. When we talk about saving money the most important thing is to understand how you earn it first. If you don't know WHEN your money is coming or WHERE it is coming from, you can't possibly plan wisely for when and what to spend.

Chapter 9

MONEY AND CREDIT

Part of the money process is understanding credit, why it is important and how it relates to your money. Credit is defined as "an arrangement by which a buyer can take possession of something now and pay for it over a period of time." Credit involves two people, the LENDER and the BORROWER. You are the borrower, and the Bank (credit card company) is the LENDER.

Credit allows you the flexibility to spend and to schedule when your payment is due, which is called CASH FLOW MANAGEMENT. In addition, everyone loves to earn cash back and mileage rewards.

NOW is the time to start getting into the conversation of credit and using your money wisely.

Credit can help if you need money for emergencies such as illness, accidents, or unexpected expenses. Credit can also function as a way to pay for necessities such as groceries, gasoline, or car repairs. Credit can also hurt you if you spend more than you can repay.

Credit is borrowed money, pure and simple. You agree to pay back the amount you borrowed plus interest and finance charges. Interest and finance charges add up quickly, and people often get themselves into financial trouble when they owe more than they can pay, when their debts outweigh their income. You want to be sure you are always able to keep up with your payments on your credit cards. Credit cards are a fast and convenient way to borrow and spend money, which makes them one of the easiest ways to get into debt trouble.

Your financial health is often expressed by one number – your Credit Score. Your Credit Score is the REPORT CARD of your credit. It shows lenders how responsibly you have managed loans, lines of credit, and your financial obligations over a period of time. Your credit history is a record of your credit life and how well you manage money. Most importantly your credit score stays with you FOREVER. If you make any mistake, something as simple as moving and forgetting to pay a credit card for 2 months, or not paying your final water/electric bill, you may not be able to remove that error for SEVEN years. So, if you make a mistake in college, it may stay with you until you are 30. If you think a small issue like going to collections for a $120.00 medical bill or utility bill won't hurt you, think again. It can be the difference between being able to rent an apartment or not. YES, prospective apartment landlords will check your credit; prospective employers will check your credit. It is away to gauge how fiscally responsible you are, whether you like it or not.

Also, you need to have good credit scores because good credit is necessary to make major purchases such as a car or a house or to get the BLACK CENTURION CARD.

The Mystery of your Credit Report

We have all seen the commercials for Credit Karma or for the "free credit scores." Those commercials are not being shown to sell you something but to warn you about ignoring your credit. Your credit score can change almost daily, whenever there are any changes to your credit including balance on a card, late payments, "running" your credit for a car loan, apartment or house loan, even in the store when you get a discount for "opening a credit card" with that store. Credit scores are affected by Payment History, Amounts Owed, Length of Credit History, Types of Credit Used, and New Credit.

Your Payment History – this represents is up to 40% of your overall rating:

- The number of loan and credit accounts you have paid on time.
- The number of accounts you are currently at least 30 days behind payment.
- If you have been bankrupt or had accounts sent to collections.
- How many days any delinquent accounts are past due.
- Dollar amounts past due or sent to collections.

If you have failed to make payments as agreed with your lender, your credit score will show that.

What you OWE: This accounts for at least 30% of your credit score. It indicates if you are likely to face serious financial problems in the future. This part of your score is based upon:

- The number of accounts you carry a balance on.
- How much credit you use every month. It is extremely important that you do not "Max Out" your cards.
- How much you owe on existing credit cards or loans.

New Credit: This section reflects your recent financial activity and predicts how you will behave with your credit in the future. It includes:

- How many loans or new credit cards you have opened in recent months.
- How long it's been since you opened your newest account.
- The number of times you've applied for credit in the past 12 months. (sometimes called a "hard pull")
- How long it has been since your last credit inquiry.

It is good to monitor your credit score just like the commercials on TV say you should. There are three major credit reporting agencies – Equifax, Experian, and TransUnion. You can get your score for free online, or you can subscribe for monthly monitoring, which, in today's world of Identity Theft can be extremely useful.

A good credit standing also extends beyond purchases because your credit information may be used by potential employers and landlords as a part of approving you or denying you. As mentioned above, credit is not only the borrowing of money on a credit card; it is also your financial status and reputation.

There are four types of credit:

Revolving Credit - (like a Southwest Airlines Visa Card) A bank will give you a card with a maximum credit limit, and you can only make charges up to that limit. Each month you can pay off the full balance, however, if you don't pay off the balance in full, you will need to make a minimum payment, which will include interest/ finance charges. You can improve and build your credit score as you use and pay your charges. Most credit cards are of this type, but also the ones that get you in trouble the fastest.

Charge Cards - (like the Centurion/Black card from American Express)– You can use charge cards the same way you use a Revolving Credit card, but you must pay the total balance due every month.

Service Credit - These are your service providers: utility company for electricity, Phone Company, gym memberships, water bill, etc. You receive a monthly bill for services provided. If you have bad credit, it can mean that you have to give them a deposit to secure your future uses.

Installment Credit - Car loans and house mortgages are two good examples of Installment Credit. You receive a loan for a certain amount of money, and you must repay that loan with a regular (fixed or variable) monthly payment, plus interest, over a certain period of time.

Finally, there are two categories of credit: secured and unsecured. Secured credit is a loan backed by an asset or collateral, such as real estate, your home, your car. Unsecured credit is a loan with no collateral, like credit cards, medical bills, service bills, and student loans.

Why is it helpful to have good credit? Credit is how lenders view who you are and what kind of financially responsible borrower you are. If you have always paid with cash, you actually have no credit history at all. Having no credit history can make lenders wary of you. No credit history can make you the "odd man out" in society. It may seem backwards, but no credit history can be as negative as bad credit history.

If you don't have credit now, it could be a wise idea to develop a good credit history. It's always difficult because it's the "catch 22." No one will give you credit unless you have a credit score, but you cannot get your credit score without credit. Sometimes the best way is to start with a low balance credit card (if you are under 21, you may have to find a student credit card.) Once you have a job and are earning income, you can try to get a car loan. Keep your payments steady and up-to-date. Pay off your credit cards. Be responsible and credit wise.

Now that we have talked about budgets and credit, we can talk about how both affect the two likely biggest purchases of your life, your car and your house. Let's say you wish to buy a house. Obviously, you need to ask yourself "how much house can I afford"? You must realize that money spent on a house requires a lot more than just paying the mortgage. There are utility and maintenance bills, property taxes, and homeowner's insurance requirements as well. A basic mortgage number can quickly escalate with additional fees. Upkeep can be more than your mortgage. The maintenance on a 5,000 square foot house on an acre of land can be as much as $5,000 per month. The bigger the house the higher the maintenance bills will be. (See the Appendices for the list and complications of buying a home or car.)

Thanks to MTV Cribs, houses have become physical representations of a person's wealth and success. They can also be representations of a person's personality in a way that showcases how they want to be perceived. Beware of such thinking.

Chapter 10

RISK AND REWARD

How do you prepare for the day of post career retirement? How do you plan for your financial future when your stream of income changes? A good way to do this is through investing your present money with financial strategies that will match with your future anticipated needs whether it is income or growth of value for the future.

These strategies include investing in stocks and bonds, (which can be Mutual Funds, Exchange-traded funds, or other similar related investments.) It can be as simple as a savings plan while you play. Keeping money in cash is not a bad idea if you cannot afford the risk of your investments to go down in value, rather you cannot afford the time to wait for it to recover.

Other investments may include real estate or even more exotic investments like precious metals (gold/silver), Private Equity Funds, jewelry, cars, or artwork.

A "dictionary definition" of investing is "the act of committing money or capital to an endeavor with the expectation of obtaining an additional income or profit." Renowned investor Warren Buffett simply defines investing as "the process of laying out money now to receive more money in the future."

There are always risks in investing. The value of stocks and bonds fluctuate on a daily basis. Real estate can decrease in value with changes in the market. There are always inherent risks of your investment losing money in the future.

Everyday life is filled with risks. But in some cases, you can purchase insurance to protect you from the risk. Homeowners insurance, for instance, will protect you if your house catches fire, or auto insurance in the case of an auto accident.

While there is no insurance policy against losing the value of investments, you can manage your risks through proper planning.

What is "risk?"

It is a chance of something going wrong. For health insurance, it is a risk the health insurance company takes that you will get sick or injured. In car insurance, it is the risk that your auto insurance company takes that your car will be damaged. In homeowners' insurance, it is a risk of a fire, or that a tree will fall on your house during a storm. In investing, it is the possibility you will lose money or value.

"The bigger risk, the bigger reward"

Most sports have high risk levels of injuries, but they also have a high reward level of compensation paid to athletes. Arizona Cardinal Larry Fitzgerald's 2018 salary was $11 million. LeBron James of the Los Angeles Lakers 2018 salary was $35.65 million. Seattle Seahawks' quarterback Russell Wilson presently has career earnings of $74.36 million over seven seasons. High risks and high rewards.

What is your willingness to accept RISK? Determining what your level of tolerance, your "acceptable" risk related to your investments is determining your "risk tolerance." It can be Low,

High, or Middle, and anywhere on a scale from 1 to 10.

Understanding what risk tolerance means is important before you consider investing. Perhaps you invest $50,000.00 in stocks and your $50,000.00 falls to $10,000.00. Do you have the ability to be "ok" with that drop in investment, knowing that it may recover, or it may not and you may have to reevaluate your investment strategy? Can you afford a PERMANENT loss of that one investment?

Risk levels can be divided into four categories from highest risk to lowest risk, as follows:

- Speculative – Junk Bonds, collectibles, options, futures
- Growth – Real Estate, Mutual Funds, Variable Annuities
- Income – Corporate Bonds, Preferred Stock, Treasury or Government Bonds
- Savings – Cash, Savings bonds, Fixed Annuities, Money Market Accounts

To understand the complexities of each of the above investments is not the critical point here. What is essential is that you have a basic understanding that every investment has some risk, and you understand that there are different levels of risk associated with each investment. These are discussions that should be had with your advisors over and over until you understand "where's my money, dude" as Kareem mentioned. Mutual funds are a common type of investment. They allow the investor to share in the expertise of the fund manager to pick and choose stocks and bonds within the fund. The mutual fund collects investment dollars from many investors for the purpose of investing in stocks, bonds or other assets depending on the "fund." There can be Stock Funds, Bond Funds, Gold Funds and a host of other investment portfolio choices. While mutual funds allow you to determine a specific level of risk based on the type of fund you choose, your return, just like the stock market, is not guaranteed. In addition, mutual funds can be subject to management fees that create a high cost to own.

As I am NOT an investment advisor, I will not be giving you a full explanation of different investments, but I will try to give you an overview of Stocks and Bonds. Let's look at bonds first.

When you buy a bond, you are actually loaning your money to a Company, like (General Electric) or a City, State or the Federal government. For example, the City of Phoenix may want to expand their light rail, build a hospital or other municipal improvement. So, they issue a bond to sell to investors and pay interest to those investors at a stated percentage on the bond. For example, a city issued bond may be a 10-year bond. Every year for 10 years the City of Phoenix pays you interest on the bonds you bought. If you bought a municipal bond for $100,000.00. You gave the city $100,000.00 of your money. The city pays you 6% or $6,000.00 interest every year. At the end of 10 years your interest would amount to $60,000.00. Also, at the end of 10 years the city would repay you your initial investment of $100,000.00. At the end of 10 years, your initial investment of $100,000.00 will have had a return of $160,000.00.

Bonds tend to be a desirable investment if you are looking for INCOME, as they have a set amount of interest that you are paid on a monthly or annual basis. Bond value, however, can fluctuate as interest rates on other bonds change. As long as you don't sell the bond or the bond is not called back by the issuer, you will continue to receive the interest regularly. One of the risks with bonds is that they can be "called" back by the issuer, which means that they pay you back your initial investment before the 10 years. While you will get paid your original investment, you now have $100,000 that you need to reinvest, and you no longer have that $6,000 per year of interest income.

Stocks are another type of investment. Stocks are issued by companies to raise money in order to grow their business or to undertake new projects. You may have heard that buying stocks means you buy part ownership of a company or corporation. When you purchase stock in a company, what you actually buy is a share of the capital the company uses to operate. You are giving the company money to continue to operate, and you "share" in the company's profits. That is why stocks are also called "shares" and why you, as a stockholder, are also a "shareholder."

Some companies periodically will pay out profits to their shareholders in the form of a dividend. Before you buy a company's stock, you may want to know if that company pays out dividends so that you can match it with your goals of GROWTH OR INCOME.

If you want periodic payment returns on your stock, you should buy stock in a company that pays out dividends. Whether or not you want to receive periodic dividends, the value of your stock rises and falls with the profits of the company.

You want to be certain you follow your trusted investment advisor's advice closely.

Chapter 11

What if I Don't Go Pro

I don't quote the above to discourage you but to make sure that, no matter what, you plan during your collegiate career for the moment when you become an ex-athlete.

Previously, I mentioned your transition from athlete to civilian life. The dictionary defines transition as "a process or period in which something undergoes a change and passes from one state, stage, form, or activity to another." You will eventually undergo a change from being an athlete to a second career.

Transition – change – can sometimes be difficult for anybody who's been doing the same thing for a number of years. What we do for much of our lives can define us and who we are. You meet someone at a party, and you say, "Glad to meet you. What do you do?" "Oh," they may reply, "I'm a Doctor." Or "I'm a Police officer." Or "I'm a teacher." We closely identify ourselves with our professions. Our professions become part of us, and when we undergo a change from our professions, many times it feels as if our inner selves change also. Irrationally, we may feel like a shell of our former selves.

If transition comes abruptly through an injury, being released from a team, or not being signed as a free agent, the process is no different than being fired from any job. Getting fired happens quickly and no matter how well prepared you are, (or even how much you say "I hate this job, I wish they would fire me,)" it can be a stunner. As a collegiate athlete, you may know that your athletic career is coming to a close, or you may hope that you get drafted, only to be left undrafted. If you are lucky enough to become a professional athlete, your career will still end at one point, and you must have a plan in place when that ending comes. You want to have your backup plan ready to go when your change happens, whether that change is abrupt and unexpected or whether you play to the end of a long career.

Of the NCAA student athletes,
Percentages that go pro in the US (NCAA, 2017)

Baseball 9.1%
Men's Basketball 1.1%
Women's Basketball .09%
Hockey 5.6%
Soccer 1.6%
Football 1.5%

This is a good time for a reminder of what Taylor Pak said in her book "Fit for Business,"

> "It's fair to say that the recruiting process is equitable to the job search, which means that student athletes already have a great deal of practice. Finding the right home for your unique personality and skill set is not an easy task. It takes research (again lots of research) and some time to figure out what your strengths and weaknesses are."

Transitioning from athlete to civilian life takes an average of three years for most athletes. Whether collegiate or professional, this is all you have done since you were a young child. For professional athletes, those three years are when most financial problems occur. ESPN and Sports Illustrated provided statistics that 78% of former professional athletes ran into financial issues during those first three years. Usually, those problems and issues arise because the athlete did not have a financial plan already in place before his or her transition happened. Even if you have a plan in place, adjusting to your new civilian life can be difficult. Suddenly your schedule is not what it had been for years. Suddenly your life is no longer scheduled for you. You are now 100% in control of your life, and that's not something most athletes are used to.

I have spoken to many former professional athletes regarding their transition experience, and I find a common thread for all athletes. (this is very similar to Military to Civilian life)

1. Year ONE - Most have discussed how the first year is taken up by merely adjusting to the fact they are no longer on a team, for some it was still training to get "back in the game" or waiting for the call that did not come.

2. Year TWO is spent in evaluating their options, finishing school if they did not have their degree and investigating potential jobs.

3. Year THREE is spent executing the plan.

This chapter is about the transition. Your goal is to understand how to psychologically prepare yourself for when your athletic career ends before it ends. That can be a tough challenge for any collegiate or professional athlete because you are expected to train to be the best athlete possible. It's a challenge to think about life after sport because you have to concentrate on practice every day (and school if you are a Collegiate Athlete) and prepare for game day. Somehow you must learn to balance your concentration on your present career with your consideration of your future one.

My interviews have a common response. There WILL come a time when there is no one telling you to get up, where to be, when to be where, when practice is, when dinner is, when and where the meeting is, and telling you it's lights out, "bed check." Basically, someone else has scheduled your life as an athlete for ten, fifteen, or more years. The point most former athletes make is that if you think it's hard being on a schedule, it's harder not to be. Adjusting to life without restrictions can be as hard as adjusting to strict ones, and you must be mentally prepared to understand your life will be very different when your athletic career ends.

As a highly performing athlete, you probably have been "playing your game" for a long time, perhaps since you were eight or ten years old. As a child, adults "scheduled" your life at home and at school. In college you had to follow a schedule of classes and your team's schedule. As a professional athlete, you also are following your coach's and your team's rigid schedule. When your athletic career is over, there is no one to schedule your life but yourself. You are free. You don't have to maintain a schedule if you don't want to. You can stay out all night and sleep all day. Many times, this is when depression will hit former athletes. To follow a schedule means you are more in control of your life than if you do not follow a schedule.

Unless you have a transition plan in place for your life, when you come to the end of your athletic career, you come to your "What do I do now?" moment. If you are in your 20's or 30's, your "What do I do now?" question is a question of "What do I do for the next 40 or 50 years?"

It is for this reason that you should start building the tools necessary to survive post career NOW.

Start using the tools and advantages you have as an athlete to do what we talked about in the other chapters. Build your brand. Network. Investigate and ask questions. You may not find the answer now, but you will have a good head start.

What profession would you like to be in? Once you decide, start moving in the direction of where you want to go. For example, if you would like to be in broadcasting, begin making acquaintances, network, take workshops, or intern with a network. This goes back to networking. Network with as many people as you can in whatever profession you are interested in for when your athletic career is done.

A good "tool" to have in preparing yourself for your transition is a personal mission statement. Whatever it is you want to do after your athletic career, whatever it is you want to be, it is good to know and understand what your personal mission is. It is good to begin working with your mission statement as soon as you can before the end of your athletic career. Start planning now. Set your goals. That's what a mission statement is. It's setting and defining your goals you want to attain.

What type of industries interest you? Research and use your network of people to find resources in those industries. Perhaps in the off-season volunteer as an intern to do work in something that interests you. Volunteering is a great foot-in-the-door strategy.

What is it that you want to accomplish? What is it you want to leave behind as your legacy? What are your core values? Your personal mission statement helps guide you in the direction you want to go. It helps you to think more deeply about your life, clarify your purpose, and identify what is truly important to you.

Why do you need a personal mission statement? To determine the direction in which you want to go. Writing a mission statement is an act of self-discovery. Some examples of personal mission statements are:

- Oprah Winfrey – "To be a teacher. And to be known for inspiring my students to be more than they thought they could be."
- Richard Branson, multi-millionaire founder of The Virgin Group – "To have fun in my journey through life and learn from my mistakes."
- Denise Morrison, CEO of Campbell Soup Company – "To serve as a leader, live a

balanced life, and apply ethical principles to make a significant difference."

- Microsoft – "Our mission is to empower every person and every organization on the planet to achieve more."
- Google – "To organize the world's information and make it universally accessible and useful."

Five questions to ask yourself in crafting your personal mission statement are:

- What is important and valuable to me?
- Where do I want to go in my life?
- What does "the best" look like to me?
- How do I want people to describe me?
- What kind of legacy do I want to leave behind?

Keep your statement short. Remember your statement is just as much about the people you want to impact as it is about yourself. Share your statement with trusted friends and family who might provide you with valuable insights about yourself and your statement. Don't be afraid to make changes, because as you grow and evolve, your mission may also. As a successful professional athlete, you have an opportunity to give back to your community. Perhaps that idea could be part of your mission statement also.

When you consider what your mission statement will be, there is an acronym or abbreviation that may help you. It is S.M.A.R.T. You want a "smart" statement. Those letters stand for:

S – Specific. Be specific in stating your goals.

M – Measurable. Set limits to your goals. Make them something you can do.

A – Achievable. Make your goals something you can achieve.

R – Relevant. Make your goals logical to you.

T – Time Bound. Set a target date to reach your goal. Making your goals "Time

Bound" sets a timeline to prevent procrastination.

Finally, what skills do you have that can help you in your transition to your new life? What is your personality? How have you gotten along with your teammates, front office staff, and coaches? How do you handle wins and losses? Possibly one of the best skills you can develop while a professional athlete is the skill of handling adversity.

In her book Fit for Business, Taylor Pak discusses that during most of your collegiate athletic career you have been gaining all the necessary experiences to develop a skillset that is perfect for the business world. "Athletes are capable professionals that all have the key qualities to succeed in life. By the time their collegiate sports careers are over, athletes will have spent countless hours training and investing their time in a sport that, up until this point, has very much defined their existence." She goes on to say that her entire life had been about her identity as an athlete. She states that what she "learned during the game" prepared her for life "after the game".

Taylor and Ogilvie (1984) in the Journal of Applied Sports Psychology, introduced the conceptual model of transition. The Society for Sport, Exercise and Performance Psychology newsletter issue from May 2016 talks about TRANSFERRABLE SKILLS that include the ability to perform under pressure, problem solving, organizational skills, ability to meet deadlines and challenges, setting and achieving goals, dedication, self-motivation and team related interpersonal skills.

Floyd Little, NFL Hall of Famer, says that all collegiate athletes have the keys to success, and they are Drive, Determination, Dedication, Desire, Commitment and Sacrifice.

For example, losing a big game by one point and having to go back the coming weekend and play again before the home crowd is really no different than working really hard to make a sale and losing it or spending hours developing a wonderful marketing presentation and losing the client you were trying to win. They are both losses involving adversity or unfavorable and unpleasant experiences.

A player who was been traded during his career to more than just a few teams told me that the experience allowed him to be able to integrate into any team. It was, he said, no different than stepping into a new job in a new office and learning to work with new co-workers. Additionally, with new coaches and new teams came a new "system" that he had to learn. I, while in the business world, his skill and ability to learn an entirely new playbook meant he feel comfortable learning a new company's business methods.

Another great transitional skill you have learned as a professional athlete is striving for a goal. As a team member, you wanted your team to win. Therefore, you have the skill of being competitive. You want yourself and your business team to achieve the goals you have set for yourself and the ones your business team has set for itself.

Most of all, as an athlete, you want to continually improve your skills and your game. "Better today than yesterday." You can transfer that skill, that mindset, into the business world as you transition from your old life to your new one.

Thoughts, Takeaways, and Questions

1. If I was NOT an athlete, what would I want to be?

2. What are the necessary steps to achieve that goal?

3. List 5 things that you have learned during your athlete career.

4. List 3 events that you experienced that make you a great employee.

APPENDIX I

Mentorship
Excerpts from thebalancesmb.com "the value of a business-mentor" (Allen/2018) and Virgin. com's "10 tips to becoming perfect business mentor"

Learn Why Every Entrepreneur Should Have a Business Mentor

Your friends and family, the online gurus, publications, and even casual acquaintances can provide you with a steady flow of information regarding news, industry developments, and opportunities. Industry analysts, consultants, employees, and good networking contacts can share their expert knowledge with you regarding particular situations and needs you may encounter. However, only a business mentor can truly share wisdom with you on an ongoing basis, and in a manner that can have a direct positive impact on the growth of your business over time.

The generic business advice you'll get from online publications will only go so far, and a good business mentor picks up right where that leaves off.

A business mentor is someone with more entrepreneurial business experience than you, who serves as a trusted confidante over an extended period of time, usually free of charge.

Does this sound a little too good to be true? Well, first and foremost, being a business mentor to an up-and-coming entrepreneur is a great way of giving back to their community, and to society at large when their advice and guidance can have a measurable impact helping their mentees.

Many business mentors may advise people in order to develop their skills as a teacher, manager, strategist, or consultant. Moreover, a true mentorship relationship also works in both directions—your mentor gets to learn about new ideas, strategies and tactics from you, just as you'll learn timeless wisdom from them.

Here are five key benefits of finding a business mentor:

1. Where else are you going to turn?

Once you launch into your own business, there's no boss to turn to for advice or direction when you're in a pinch—maybe not even any employees yet. Although you're flying solo, you don't have to be. Everybody needs a good reliable sounding board, second opinion, and sometimes just emotional support when the times get tough (which they will).

2. They've "been there and done that."

Perhaps the most obvious benefit of finding a business mentor is that you can learn from their previous mistakes and successes. Your mentor doesn't need to have experience in your particular industry—though it helps if they do—so that you're maximizing your opportunities to leverage key relationships. They don't have to be up on the latest trends or technology—you've got other sources for that. Your mentor's role is to share with you lessons from their experience in the hopes that you can learn them quickly and easily.

3. It's (usually) free.

If you're on a tight budget, that's a major factor. While good coaches and consultants may be able to offer some things that a mentor doesn't, it almost always comes at a price, usually of several hundred dollars (or more) each month. Mentors, though, are readily available, free of charge through a number of organizations, such as SCORE (Service Corps Of Retired Executives) and many other groups. Plan on at least treating your mentor to lunch or coffee when you meet together.

4. Expand your social network.

Your mentor, being an experienced businessperson, is likely to have an extensive network, and can offer you access to far more senior decision-makers than you currently have. They will be far more willing to open that network up to you than some casual acquaintance from a networking meeting.

5. A trusted, long-term relationship.

Your mentor has no ulterior motive—no service or product to sell you. That, combined with their experience, creates a good foundation for trust. And as the relationship develops over time, that trust can grow even stronger. Also, your time with them becomes more and more efficient as they become more and more familiar with you and your business.

As you can see, the rewards are potentially great to bring on a business mentor, and the risk is non-existent. You have nothing to lose and everything to gain by finding a good mentor. Every entrepreneur should have one.

There's a decline in the number of businesses starting up in the United States as we see the economy improving. This means less people are starting businesses out of necessity, and instead people are doing so out of passion and because they see an opportunity in the market.

Programs like The Presidential Ambassadors for Global Entrepreneurship are focused on developing the next generation of entrepreneurs, but what can we individually do to help? You may know someone who is interested in starting their own business or embodies the entrepreneurial spirit – perhaps an intern or employee at your company, your neighbor, maybe even your child. Here are some suggestions on how to work with the next generation to set them up for success as a business owner.

While starting a business out of passion rather than necessity sets one up for success initially, the fact remains that many entrepreneurs lack the basic business or leadership skills that are necessary to maintain or grow a business. We see new businesses fail all the time, and the majority of the time it's due to incompetence.

1. Communication – Being able to communicate effectively will help build relationships, problem solve, and convey what a business is and why consumers need whatever is being sold. Unfortunately, many young people are lacking at face-to-face interactions because of social media and text messages. Successful businesses require that people actually speak to one another.

Start with the importance of a professional appearance and introductions (eye contact, handshake) and the importance of the elevator speech. As an entrepreneur, they'll likely have to pitch their business and it's got to be on point in order to compete.

2. Leadership – Look for opportunities to put them in charge. The bottom line is that an entrepreneur is their own boss, and might eventually be the manager of other people. They need to have experience taking ownership of things and making decisions.

3. Goal setting – Have a conversation to understand what the individual aspires to be. Jot down

several goals and have them pick the one that makes the most sense to be their main focus. Figure out what steps are necessary to accomplish this goal and encourage them to start taking action on those steps immediately. Remember, goals can be altered and now's the perfect time to lay some groundwork for a future business.

4. Recognize opportunities – Teaching future entrepreneurs to seek out opportunities and act on them will directly contribute to their level of future success. Encourage young people to point out small problems or setbacks in their lives or at work. Brainstorm solutions on how to resolve their troubles. This will teach them to focus on creating positive solutions, instead of focusing on the problem itself.

5. Failure – we're often taught that failure is unacceptable. When it comes to entrepreneurship, failure can be a positive thing if there is a lesson learned. Budding entrepreneurs need to understand that at some point, something is not going to go their way – it's part of owning a business.

It's important to be resilient and learn from the situation so they grow as an individual and make better business decisions in the future.

6. Giving back – Every entrepreneur hopes to be successful one day. Understanding the importance of giving back will help the next generation stay humble during periods of success and it will teach them that a successful business provides benefits to more than just its owner.

7. Independence – Having the freedom to make your own decisions is often considered to be one of the greatest benefits of entrepreneurship. The key to independence is confidence. In many cases, confidence must be learned. In the case of a future entrepreneur, they're going to learn to believe in their own abilities from acting on challenges, seeing the results and being praised and respected by others.

8. Financial literacy – This is one area where entrepreneurs really struggle. It's one thing to manage your own bank account, but what about managing the money coming in and out of a business? At work, let an aspiring entrepreneur co-own the department's budget. It's also a good idea to prep them for the fact that they will likely need help in this area; an accountant can serve as an advisor on where a business's money is going vs. where it should be going.

APPENDIX II

Money and Credit

Why Budget?

- Helps you to live within your means and meet expenses
- Helps you save for long- and short-term goals
- Giving you goals to achieve and monitor

Why Save?

- In case of an emergency
- To take advantage of opportunities
- To reach financial goals

The Debit Card

- ATM Card bit with Bank logo
- Looks just like a credit card, but not a loan, no interest

- Backed only by the checking account behind it
- Widely accepted, can be a good budgeting tool
- Immediate use of money, make sure you don't go overdraft.

When to Use Debit Card vs Credit Card vs Cash

- How you spend money for everyday expenses like groceries, gas, movie theatres and restaurants, clothing should be part of an "overall" spending and savings plan to keep you on track.

Your Credit Score

- Everything you do with your credit accounts affects your credit score including car and school loan
- Creditors extend credit to credit worthy customers
- When you pay your bills on time, you are proving yourself credit worthy

Banks reward good customers with lower interest rate loans and higher credit lines

- Employers may check your score. A bad score may result in fewer job offers
- Non-installment credit

  - Regular
  - 30-day charge accounts (American Express)
  - Travel and entertainment cards

- Installment credit

  - Car loan, student loan, home loan
  - Furniture purchase

- Revolving credit

  - Department store cards
  - Bank cards: Visa/MasterCard

THREE factors that your Credit Score Says about you

Character – how well you handle financial obligations

Capital – the assets you own, including real estate, savings and investments

Capacity – how much debt you can manage based upon your income

Character

Character is an evaluation of how likely you are to repay your debts. Potential lenders look at your past history, including:

- How well you've handled your money in the past.
- Did you pay bills on time?
- Have you ever filed for bankruptcy?
- How long have you lived at your present address?
- How long have you been at your present job?

Capacity

Capacity looks at how much debt you can handle based on your current financial situation. Lenders want to know whether or not you have been working regularly in a job that will provide enough income to support your credit use.

- Do you have a steady job or income?
- How much do you earn?
- How many other loan payments do you have?
- What are your current living expenses?
- What other debts do you have?

- ○ Do you have children or other dependents that you are supporting?

Advantages of being creditworthy:

- ○ You are more likely to secure favorable rates on loans and credit accounts
- ○ You may qualify for lower auto insurance rates
- ○ You will be able to open utility accounts for your apartment or house without paying large deposits

Challenges of **NOT** being considered creditworthy:

- ○ You will not be able to get loans or credit cards
- ○ You will be charged higher loan and credit card interest rates
- ○ You may be rejected in favor of candidates with better credit histories when you apply to rent an apartment

APPENDIX III

The power of SAVING

1. Simple interest

Principal x interest rate x time = interest earned

$100,000 x .05 x 1 = $5000 interest earned every year

2. Compound interest

When your interest compounds, it gets added back to your account and becomes part of your principal. With more principal, the account earns even more interest, which continually compounds into new principal. It's a powerful cycle that really adds up.

In the simple interest example above, $100,000 at a 5% simple APR, earns $5000 in interest every year.

However, if that interest compounds once a year, the $5000 interest you earn in year one would be added to the principal at the beginning of year two. By doing this, you earn more interest in year two ($5,250.) and even more in every subsequent year.

$100,000 x .05 x 1 = $5000 interest earned in year one
$100,050 x .05 x 1 = $5250 interest earned in year two

The Rule of 72 – Double Down

How fast can your money DOUBLE? The Rule of 72 is a fast way to estimate how long it will take you to double your savings with compound interest. How it is calculated:

72 divided by the interest rate = the number of years needed to double your money. Therefore, if you have a 10% interest rate and want to know how long it will take to double your money, the equation would be:
72 divided by 10 = 7.2 years

APPENDIX IV

Advisors

1. Lawyer (JD)

    ○ Estate Planning- protection for Probate, Creditors, execute your wishes
    ○ Asset Protection – protection from Creditors
    ○ Litigation – You sue someone or someone sues you
    ○ Intellectual Property – setup and protect your brand
    ○ Business Attorney – regular operations of a business, documents and compliance with state and federal laws

American Bar Association Service Center – to find your local state bar
(800) 285-2221
[International (312) 988-5000]

https://www.americanbar.org/about_the_aba/
contact/

2. Investment Advisor (CFP, ChFA, etc)
   ◦ Choosing the right investments
   ◦ Education you on what you are investing in and why
   ◦ Planning for Long Term and Short Term
   ◦ May also help with
      ◦ Life Insurance
      ◦ Disability Insurance
      ◦ Long Term Care Insurance

FINRA Investor Complaint Center
http://www.finra.org/
9509 Key West Avenue
Rockville, MD 20850-3329
Phone: (240) 386-HELP (4357)

Problems addressed by FINRA:

   ◦ Buy or sell orders
   ◦ Brokerage firm or broker
   ◦ Insider trading
   ◦ Manipulation of security price or volume
   ◦ Account transfer
   ◦ 401(k), pension or retirement plan
   ◦ Investment adviser/financial planner

- ○ Other - Complaints other than those noted in the sections below

3. Certified Public Accountant (CPA)
   - ○ Taxes, Taxes and more Taxes
   - ○ Business Structure
   - ○ Business Plan development
   - ○ Business management
   - ○ Personal CFO
   - ○ Business Consulting and Planning

NASBA – National Associations of the State Board Of Accountants
To find your local state board https://nasba.org/
150 Fourth Ave. North, Ste. 700
Nashville, TN 37219-2417
Phone: (615) 880-4200

APPENDIX V

Goal Setting

Before the start of the season, before the start of any game, before the start of an athletic career, you set goals. Win the Stanley Cup, Super Bowl, World Series, NBA champs, Gold Medals or NCAA Championships, those are goals! They are concrete and the path to get achieving them is pretty straight forward. Those are team goals. While the Olympics may be individual goals, it still resonates as a goal for the Olympic Team or your Country. Individual goals may be a number of Wins, Hits, Goals, Touchdowns, etc.

Goals for professionals, entrepreneurs, or employees may be slightly less concrete or the path may be indirect. If your goal is to be the CFO of a Publicly Traded company, that is a lofty and achievable goal; however, the path to get there may be direct or may take thousands of little goals.

What about FINANCIAL GOALS?

Basic financial goals revolve around money. Getting it (Earnings), Keeping it (Saving), using it wisely (Budgets), growing it (investments) or giving it away (Charity.) Any way you want to set your goals there is no right or wrong answer.

How to set your goals is up to you. Who helps you process your desires and wishes, who helps you achieve them, what they are, is ALL up to you.

Once you set your goals, how you get there is the challenge. Start by working backward. If your goal is to hit .300 in baseball, then start with what is my batting average today. Next, you need to consult with experts on how to improve your batting stance, swing, mental approach to the plate, how you perform against certain teams, pitchers, stadiums, weather etc.

Harvey Mackay recently published an article in his syndicated column that 'Goals require growth to be achieved." He has his own formula for goals.

- Make it Positive - don't set your goal to be "not to strike out so much."
- Be fully Committed.

- Step By Step – By working with your professional team, you can build a program to reach your goals. I recently sat with my investment advisor and said; "this is what I want to have when I retire, here is where I am now, how do I get there?" We then set up a 10-year plan to achieve the goal.

- Appreciate the learning experience – you may have challenges and delays or other hurdles in front of you. Figure out what does NOT work, what DOES work and why.

- Take them seriously – if you don't, no one else will either.

- Trust your judgment - In addition trust the judgment of your professional advisors/ coaches. There is NO rule against asking for help.

- BE AMBITIOUS - there is no sense in achieving a goal that does not require effort, if it seems too big, then break it up into smaller goals along your path.

Mackay's Moral: Don't be afraid to dream big – be afraid not to.

APPENDIX VI

*Large Asset Purchases – Cars and Homes
(source Visa Financial Soccer, 2012,2018)*

I did not want to overload you with too much information, so I wanted to make sure you knew how complicated and how intricate the two largest purchases you may make in your life can be.

When shopping for a car

1. Decisions
   - Deciding how much to spend (Need vs Wants)
   - How to Pay for it All Cash or Car Loan
   - Do I get New or Used?
   - How do I Finance it? Lease or Purchase

2. Private Party or Dealer or Carvana online
   - If you decide on a used car from a dealer

- ○ Consider costs, reliability, dealer reputation
- ○ Research Carfax, Edmunds, KBB etc.

3. Consider the warranty and the service contract

- ○ What to do if you have problems
- ○ A used car from a private party
- ○ Sometimes includes a manufacturer's warranty
- ○ Difference in price compared to a dealer

4. A new car

- ○ Read about new car features and prices
- ○ Shop around
- ○ Plan to negotiate price
- ○ Learn the terms
- ○ Consider the service contract

Car Loans

What to consider when shopping for a car loan

- ○ Annual Percentage Rate of Interest
- ○ Length of loan
- ○ Monthly payments
- ○ Total finance charge
- ○ Total to be repaid

- ○ Shop around for a car loan and compare the Interest Rate
- ○ What is a Lease? How is it different from a Loan/Purchase?
- ○ What is a co-signer?
- ○ Understand the circumstances under which a vehicle can be repossessed, and list the legal
- ○ Rights and responsibilities of the creditor and of the debtor

The cost to own, operate, and maintain a car

- ○ Initial purchase price
- ○ Registration and title costs
- ○ Sales tax
- ○ Financing cost
- ○ Insurance
- ○ Scheduled maintenance
- ○ Unscheduled repairs and maintenance
- ○ Gasoline, oil and other fluids
- ○ Parking and tolls

About warranties and service contracts

1. Types of warranties

- ○ As-is warranty

- ○ Implied warranty
- ○ Dealer warranty
- ○ Manufacturer's warranty

2. Service contracts

3. Preventing problems

4. Resolving disputes

5. Comparing promises of warranties and service contract

About auto insurance

1. Importance of and legal requirements

2. Types of coverage

- ○ Bodily injury liability
- ○ Property damage liability
- ○ Collision
- ○ Comprehensive
- ○ Medical payments
- ○ Uninsured motorist
- ○ Rental reimbursement
- ○ Towing and labor

3. How insurance rates are set

- ○ Age
- ○ Sex

- Marital status
- Personal habits (e.g., smoking)
- Type of use
- Frequency of use
- Location
- Driving record deductible
- Type of car
- Value and age of car

BUYING A HOME

First, SHOULD I buy or Rent
Comparing renting and buying

1. Main advantages of renting are:

- Ease of mobility – Lock it and Leave it
- Fewer responsibilities
- Lower initial costs – no cost for repairs and Maintenance

2. Common disadvantages of renting are:

- Few financial benefits in the form of tax deductions
- Restricted lifestyle, decorating, having pets, and other activities
- Legal concerns (landlords and neighbors)
- No opportunity to have the value of a home

3. Key benefits of buying your housing are:

    ◦ Tax savings
    ◦ Pride of ownership
    ◦ Potential economic gain

4. Disadvantages of buying your house may include:

    ◦ Financial risks related to having down payment funds, obtaining a mortgage, fluctuating
    ◦ property values
    ◦ Limited mobility if a home is difficult to sell
    ◦ Higher living costs due to repairs and maintenance

BUYING A HOME, The process

1. Phase 1 - How much home do you NEED vs WANT

2. Phase 2 - Location Location Location

3. Phase 3 - Finding a home within your Price

4. Phase 4 - Finance and Close

    ◦ Applying for a mortgage
        • Determine an estimated value of the house

- Obtain funds for a down payment
- Know your credit score
- Compare fees, services, and mortgage rates for different lenders
○ Prepare the mortgage application
  - types of mortgages
  - A conventional mortgage has equal payments, typically over 15, 30, or 40 years based on a fixed interest rate
  - Government-guaranteed financing programs include loans from the Federal Housing Authority (FHA) and the Veterans Administration (VA)
  - A balloon mortgage has fixed monthly payments and a very large final payment, usually after three, five, or seven years
  - The adjustable rate mortgage (ARM), also referred to as a flexible rate mortgage or a variable rate mortgage, has an interest rate that increases or decreases during the life of the loan based on changes in market interest rates
  - A graduated payment mortgage has payments rising to different levels during the term of the loan
  - An interest-only mortgage consists of interest-only payments for a specified period, usually five to ten years

- Reverse mortgages provide an elderly homeowner with tax-free income in the form of a loan that is paid back (with interest) when the home is sold or the homeowner dies
- Refinancing refers to obtaining a new mortgage on your current home at a lower interest rate

○ selecting a mortgage
  - Shop around for mortgages through multiple lenders
  - Estimate a mortgage payment based on different factors including interest rates and different terms of the loan closing costs

○ The common costs associated with the settlement of a real estate transaction may include:
  - Attorney or escrow fees
  - Title insurance
  - Property taxes
  - Appraisal fee
  - Recording fees, transfer taxes
  - Loan discount points
  - Inspections
  - Lender's origination fee
  - Reserves for home insurance and property taxes

- Interest (paid from date of closing to 30 days before first monthly payment)
- Real estate agent commission

APPENDIX VII

Starting a Business

1. How to Start a Business
   - Is Entrepreneurship For You?
   - 20 Questions Before Starting
   - 10 Steps to Starting a Business
   - Understand Your Market
     - Business Data & Statistics
     - General Business Statistics
     - Consumer Statistics
     - Demographics
     - Economic Indicators
     - Employment Statistics
     - Income Statistics
     - Money & Interest Rates
     - Production & Sales Statistics
     - Trade Statistics
     - Statistics for Specific Industries

2. Business Types
   - Green Businesses

- ○ Startups & High Growth Businesses
- ○ Home-Based Businesses
- ○ Online Businesses
- ○ Franchise Businesses
- ○ Buying Existing Businesses
- ○ Self Employed & Independent Contractors
- ○ Women-Owned Businesses
- ○ Veteran-Owned Businesses
- ○ People with Disabilities
- ○ Young Entrepreneurs
- ○ Encore Entrepreneurs
- ○ Minority-Owned Businesses
- ○ Native Americans

3. Find a Mentor or Counselor

4. Write Your Business Plan
   - ○ Executive Summary
   - ○ Company Description
   - ○ Market Analysis
   - ○ Organization & Management
   - ○ Service or Product Line
   - ○ Marketing & Sales
   - ○ Funding Request
   - ○ Financial Projections
   - ○ Appendix
   - ○ How to Make Your Business Plan Stand Out

5. Choose Your Business Structure
   - ○ Sole Proprietorship

- Limited Liability Company
- Cooperative
- Corporation
- Partnership
- S Corporation

6. Choose & Register Your Business
   - Choose Your Business Name
   - Register Your Business Name
   - Register With State Agencies

7. Choose Your Business Location & Equipment
   - Tips for Choosing Your Business Location
   - Basic Zoning Laws
   - Home-Based Business Zoning Laws
   - Leasing Commercial Space
   - Buying Government Surplus
   - Leasing Business Equipment

8. Business Licenses & Permits
   - Federal Licenses & Permits
   - State Licenses & Permits

9. Learn About Business Laws
   - Advertising & Marketing Law
   - Employment & Labor Law
   - Finance Law
   - Intellectual Property Law
   - Online Business Law
     - Collecting Sales Tax Online
     - International Online Sales
   - Privacy Law

- ○ Obtain Your Federal Business Tax ID
- ○ Determine Your Federal Tax Obligations
- ○ Determine Your State Tax Obligations
- ○ Determine When the Tax Year Starts

13. Hire & Retain Employees

Bibliography

Motley Fool.com; 6 Financial Mistakes That Are Ruining Your Credit; Kailey Fralick Jul 23; https://www.fool.com/credit-cards/2018/07/23/6-financial-mistakes-that-are-ruining-your-credit.aspx

Motley Fool.com; 3 Smart Ways to Save Money on Your Next Car; Matthew Frankel, CFP ; Sep 13, 2018; https://www.fool.com/retirement/2018/09/13/3-smart-ways-to-save-money-on-your-next-car.aspx

Investopedia.com; what is a Budget? Budgeting Terms and Tips; Reviewed by Julia Kagen ; Updated Jan 17, 2018; https://www.investopedia.com/terms/b/budget.asp

Investopedia.com; How to Find a Financial Advisor/Planner ; https://www.

investopedia.com/updates/find-financial-advisor-planner.

Investopedia.com; https://www.investopedia.com/financial-edge/0312/why-athletes-go-broke.aspx; Why Athletes Go Broke ; Tim Parker ; Mar 5, 2012

Nerdwallet ; Associated Press Former stars explain why NFL players go broke, and what you can learn;; Oct. 10, 2017 https://www.businessinsider.com/ap-liz-weston-why-nfl-players-go-broke-and-what-you-can-learn-2017-10

Investopedia.com; What do Financial Advisors Do; https://www.investopedia.com/articles/personal-finance/050815/what-do-financial-advisers-do.asp

https://www.pressreader.com/usa/the-arizona-republic/20181224/281621011449525 Dec 24, 2018 - Goals require growth to be achieved

Investopedia.com Risk Tolerance; https://www.investopedia.com/articles/pf/07/risk_tolerance.asp

Motley Fool.com; Budgeting 101: How to Start Budgeting for the First Time; Christy

Bieber; Apr 21, 2018 at 10:16AM; https://www.fool.com/investing/2018/04/21/budgeting-101-how-to-start-budgeting-for-the-first.aspx?source=isesitlnk0000001&mrr=1.00

Pacific Standard Magazine; How We Set Up Our Professional Athletes to Fail; Author: Sam Riches; Publish date:Feb 18, 2014 https://psmag.com/economics/professional-athletes-set-fail-74247

Forbes.com; Curt Schilling And Why Athletes Make Such Poor Financial Decisions; Monte Burke ; SportsMoney; May 25, 2012, 12:50pm; https://www.forbes.com/sites/monteburke/2012/05/25/curt-schilling-and-why-athletes-make-such-poor-financial-decisions/#12ddfb9531b4

American Psychological Association; Exercise and Sport Psychology Newsletter; May 2016; https://www.apa.org/about/division/div47.aspx

Floyd Little, Interview for "Beyond the Game", (Silverlight Films, 2017)

Securities and Exchange Commission; SEC.gov https://www.investor.gov/research-before-

you-invest/research/five-questions-ask-
before-you-invest

By Kareem Abdul-Jabbar; 20 Things I Wish I'd
Known When I Was 30; When I was thirty,
Apr 30, 2013; https://www.esquire.com/
news-politics/news/a22394/kareem-
things-i-wish-i-knew/

Paychex Inc; https://www.paychex.com/articles/
startup/employee-to-entrepreneur-
businesses-start;

NCAA, http://www.ncaa.org/about/resources/
research/estimated-probability-competing-
college-athletics; 2018

https://www.thebalancesmb.com/the-value-of-a-
business-mentor-1200818 (Allen/2018)

NCAA; http://www.ncaa.org/about/resources/
research/estimated-probability-competing-
professional-athletics; 2018

Michelle Gill; Value of and contributions of the
participation in intercollegiate athletics on
the personal development of community

college-aged students; (2015) http://
digitalcommons.unl.edu/cehsedaddiss/232

Pro Athletes Prove Why You Should Stick To A
Financial Playbook; Aug 16, 2017, Zach
Conway https://www.forbes.com/sites/
zachconway/2017/08/16/pro-athletes-
prove-why-you-should-stick-to-a-financial-
playbook/

college-aged students; (2015) http://
digitalcommons.unl.edu/cehsedaddiss/232

Danny Schayes; Fast Broke: Learn the reason
athletes go broke; Nomad CEO Publishing;
isbn 13:978-1502869715.

https://www.virgin.com/entrepreneur/10-tips-
becoming-perfect-business-mentor

https://www.sba.gov/business-guide/

Money 101; Visa Practical Money Skills; https://
www.practicalmoneyskills.com; (2018)

Robert Pagliarini ; Why athletes go broke: The
myth of the dumb jock; MoneyWatch;
https://www.cbsnews.com/news/why-

athletes-go-broke-the-myth-of-the-dumb-jock; (2013)

Jonathan Miller CPA; https://www.forbes.com; want-to-retire-early-take-a-cue-from-the-pro-baller-playbook. (2016)

Jonathan Miller, CPA; https://www.cnbc.con; for-athletes-like-sergio-garcia-tax-season-brings-extra-burdens (2017)

Jonathan Miller, CPA; NFL Rookie year; Life after football; Interview WBEZ; (2015) http://www.sportsfinancial.org/nfl-rookie-yearlife-after-football-wbezs-morning-shift/

Jonathan Miller, CPA; Professional Athletes Retirement Conundrum; Chief Investment Officer Magazine; http://www.ai-ciodigital.com/ai-cio; (2016)

Susan Johnson Taylor; interview with Jonathan Miller , CPA; https://money.usnews.com/money/personal-finance/articles; (2016)

22/what-pro-athletes-can-teach-us-about-retirement-planning

Amy Armstrong; The Suit Magazine; Don't Blow It; interview with Jonathan Miller, CPA (2016)

Jonathan Miller, CPA; Wall Street Journal on Advising Professional Athletes; https://www.wsj.com/articles/SB10001424127887323419604578573341985977374 via @ WSJ.

https://www.cnbc.com/2015/04/23/maybe-floyd-mayweathers-spending-is-the-key-to-winning.htmlMaybe Floyd Mayweather's spending is the key to winning; Robert Frank (2015)

Sheth, Hela & M. Babiak, Kathy. (2010). Beyond the Game: Perceptions and Practices of Corporate Social Responsibility in the Professional Sport Industry. Journal of Business Ethics. 91. 433-450. 10.1007/s10551-009-0094-0. (2010)

Babiak, Kathy & Mills, Brian & Tainsky, Scott & Juravich, Matthew. (2012). An

Investigation Into Professional Athlete Philanthropy:

www.growingagreenerworld.com/jason-brown-football-player-to-farmer/2019

https://www.sec.gov/litigation/admin/2017/34-79991.pdf

About the Authors

Jonathan Miller, CPA

Jonathan Miller is a regular consultant and speaker for NCAA and Professional athletes on finances as well as navigating the NIL World. www.starcrossllc.com

Jonathan is also a producer of the documentary co-produced and directed by Susan Sember, "Beyond the Game" began production in July 2015. Since then producers have captured hundreds of hours of footage (4K-8K) on this project here in the U.S. and abroad featuring current, retired, and future athletes, who, for the first time, shared their stories about financial struggles and success.

Jonathan Miller was graduated from the University of California, Santa Barbara with a Bachelor of Arts degree in Business Economics; Accounting emphasis, with Honors, June 1986 and passed all four parts of the uniform CPA Examination in the top 5% of the nation in May 1986. From there he proceeded to work for Arthur Young and Co. in their audit department, including the audit of a large independent film studio.

Jonathan founded StarCross Management LLC to serve his clients in the Sports and Entertainment Industry and has extensive experience in the Music and Publishing industry, including working with local start up bands as well as establish artists as well as Professional Athletes in the NHL, NFL, NBA and MLB including some international athletes in Soccer (football), MMA and the Olympics.

Jonathan has been working with High School and Collegiate athletes for the past few years helping navigate the NIL world and has been integral in the transition from College to Pro for many young athletes.

Taylor Madwin

Joining Jonathan in this journey is Taylor Madwin. Taylor is a graduate of USC and ASU's Allan "Bud" Selig Sports Law and Business program. As an avid sports fan she has an uncanny wealth of sports knowledge. Taylor has worked with the Fiesta Bowl and 2024 NCAA Final Four as a program event coordinator and hopes to expand and integrate her love of sports in her professional career.

Made in the USA
Las Vegas, NV
20 May 2024